6 SURE WAYS TO SOLVE ANY PROBLEM NO MATTER WHAT

William J. Diehm, Ph.D

BROADMAN
& HOLMAN
PUBLISHERS

Nashville, Tennessee

4260-89
0-8054-6089-6

Dewey Decimal Classification: 153.4
Subject Heading:
PROBLEM SOLVING // DECISION MAKING // CRITICAL
THINKING
Library of Congress Card Catalog Number: 93-38554
Printed in the United States of America

Scripture quotations marked (NIV) are from the Holy Bible, *New International Version,* copyright © 1978 New York International Bible Society; (NASB) are from the *New American Standard Bible,* © The Lockman Foundation, 1960, 1962, 1963, 1968, 1971, 1972, 1973, 1975, 1977; and (KJV) from the *King James Version* of the Bible.

Library of Congress Cataloging-in-Publication Data
Diehm, William J.
6 sure ways to solve any problem, no matter what / William J. Diehm
    p. cm.
ISBN 0-8054-6089-6
1. Christian life–Baptist authors. 2. Problem solving.
    I. Title. II. Title: Six sure ways to solve any problem, no matter what.
BV4501.2.D53   1994
153.4'3–dc20
                                      93-38554
                                        CIP

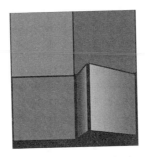

Contents

PART 3: Through the Open Door

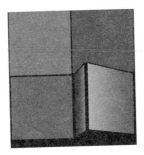

Introduction

As I was resting inside my house by the open patio door, I noticed a honey-laden bee buzzing against a windowpane, striving to get back to its hive. I folded a piece of paper and tried to guide the bee toward the open door. The more I pushed, the more it buzzed futilely against the windowpane. The next day I observed its dead, shriveled body on the windowsill. This magnificent creature of God was doomed to die just a foot away from an open door because it could not or would not back up and try another way.

We humans are the greatest problem-solving mechanisms made by the Creator. But so many of us do not use common sense or the God-given ability to solve problems. Instead, we die without hope on the windowsills of life because we don't know how to back up, move over, and choose the open door. We buzz hopelessly against the windowpane, not realizing that the open door is just a step away.

As the bee seems incapable of recognizing that it is trying to fly through an impenetrable windowpane, we humans often persevere in a windowpane direction that keeps us from problem-solving. When we recognize the deceptive windowpanes, ways that won't work to resolve problems, we can become receptive to the open doors that allow us to solve the problems of life.

We are all familiar with today's emphasis on positive thinking, but we often forget that we have no positive way of doing anything unless we are firmly grounded on what we cannot do. The Ten Commandments, "Thou shalt not" (Ex. 20:1–17, KJV), come before the Great Commission, "Thou shalt go" (Matt. 28:19, paraphrased). Unless we get some feedback on what we are doing wrong, we can never make the corrections to do right.

We are all familiar with today's emphasis on positive thinking, but we often forget that we have no positive way of doing anything unless we are firmly grounded on what we cannot do.

A blindfolded archer would never be able to hit the target unless someone told him that he was to the left, right, up, down, or facing the wrong way. The archer needs feedback. Even if he hit the target, the blind archer would not know unless someone told him. When we tackle problems, we are often like a blind archer. We need feedback which tells us what not to do in order for us to know what to do.

How to Win Friends and Influence People by Dale Carnegie is one of the most positive books ever written. Harry

O. Hamm once asked Mr. Carnegie why he chose to start his book with a negative. Carnegie replied, "There was just no other way to say, 'Don't criticize, condemn or complain,' without being negative and saying, 'Don't do it!'" And that's why the first part of the book *6 Sure Ways to Solve Any Problem No Matter What* tells us what *not* to do before we find out what *to* do.

There is just no other way to keep a person from beating his wings futilely against the windowpane (a way that looks right but through which we cannot go) but to say, "Don't do it, friend—that's a windowpane, and you can't fly that way." Happily, there are some exciting open doors, and we can succeed in going through them if we know where they are.

PART 1

Windowpanes: Unsuccessful Problem-Solving Techniques

Ignoring the Problem

Sixty-eight years ago, when I was a little boy in kindergarten, I learned about the mythical ostrich who stuck his head in the sand to avoid danger. His idea was "If I don't know about it, it won't hurt me. If I hide my head in the sand, the lion will go away." Ignoring your problem will not make the problem go away. It may make you feel better temporarily, but ignoring is not a problem-solving technique; it's a windowpane, not an open door.

There are three ways I have observed that people try to solve their problems through "The Windowpane of Ignoring": denial, repression, and undoing.

Denial

One method of ignoring a problem is the defense mechanism of denial. When I was a young man, I lived next door to a lady who believed in denial. She had an infection in her knee that caused her leg to swell to twice its normal size. She walked in great pain and anguish. One day I asked her, "What's wrong with your leg?" She looked me in the eye and bristled, "There's nothing wrong with my leg, absolutely nothing." I was always curious about what she thought when the infected leg was amputated to save her life.

Ignoring your problem will not make the problem go away. It may make you feel better temporarily, but ignoring is not a problem-solving technique; it's a windowpane, not an open door.

The first step in problem-solving is to admit that you have the problem. There is no help for the alcoholic who refuses to admit that he is an alcoholic. When the alcoholic comes to the place where he can stand up and confess before a group of people, "I am an alcoholic," he becomes receptive to help. But as long as he denies that he really does need help, I suppose he thinks, "Perhaps it will go away."

A long time ago, the Master Teacher said some words that have been engraved onto the portals of many a library: "Ye shall know the truth, and the truth shall make you free" (John 8:32, KJV). To deny the existence of a problem is an effort to make this classic verse of no avail. When we can't face the truth, we are saying, in effect, "You shall believe a lie, and the lie shall set you free."

When I worked at Terminal Island Federal Penitentiary, I conducted group therapy for inmates. When a new convict came into our group, we first had him tell the story of his arrest, conviction, and incarceration. After he finished his story, the convicts would exclaim facetiously, "And of course, you're innocent!" Until a man admitted that he was guilty, that he deserved his sentence, and that he *had* a problem, it was impossible to make any progress in group therapy.

"Yes, I did do that. Yes, I am guilty. And yes, I *do* have a problem," are the words that make "Please help me" the prelude to the solution.

The defense mechanism of denial stops us dead cold in our tracks. We can go no further; we solve no problems. But the confession, "Yes, I have a problem and here it is" opens the door to the solution to all the great problems of life.

The defense mechanism of denial is a part of the windowpane of ignoring. It successfully stops the solution to the problems of life. Don't go that way.

At one time I worked with an oncologist. He often had the ominous duty of announcing to people that they had cancer. This grim news was so frightening that roughly 10 percent of the people who heard it never went back to the doctor, hoping the cancer would go away.

Unfortunately, the problem that is not admitted and faced does not go away; it only gets worse or comes back in another form.

The defense mechanism of denial is a part of the windowpane of ignoring. It successfully stops the solution to the problems of life. Don't go that way.

Repression

The second method of ignoring is called repression, which is burying the problem deep down inside where one becomes unaware of its existence. The problem is still there—we just repress it or bury it in a level of our consciousness where we can forget about dealing with it.

Burying unsolved problems in the unconscious causes them to fester and grow. They attach themselves to other problems and form an unnatural alliance. Problems follow the natural inclination of the human to organize. A group of organized problems buried deep within harms the mind more than the Mafia harms our communities. Problems can organize and attack us as a guerrilla movement. We go along blithely until one day they hit us and knock us flat. That is why many people are trying to heal their memories.

The central part of the United States is called "Tornado Alley." Researchers Sims and Bauman discovered that more people were killed at the southern end of Tornado Alley than at the northern end. They found that the deaths were not caused by population density or the severity of the storms or the construction of the homes, but by the mental attitude of the people who lived in the south. The southerners in this study were more frequently "externalizers" who saw themselves being manipulated by external forces beyond their control. This attitude led them to respond to the threat of a tornado by folding their hands and awaiting their destiny.

They coped with stress by ignoring the existence of the danger. That's repression.

King David, ruler of ancient Israel, had a deep faith in God. He penned the words, "Yea, though I walk through the valley of the shadow of death, I will fear no evil: for thou art with me" (Ps. 23:4, KJV). Yet, when his enemies chased him, he ran to protect himself. A person can have a deep faith in God without being fatalistic. To say "Nothing will happen to me; God will take care of me," and then take a nap in the middle of the freeway, is to close our eyes to the responsibility the Creator delegated to us. Jesus said, "Thou shalt not tempt the Lord thy God" (Matt. 4:7, KJV).

When we ignore our problems, we put God to a test. When we repress our problems or deny their existence, they are never solved; they only fester.

Many people say to me, "I don't know what's wrong. I feel so unhappy and restless and upset. I wonder, am I having a nervous breakdown?" Those comments let me know that the person has repressed one problem too many. Their problems are now in the process of robbing them of the joy of living.

An unsolved problem is like an unpaid debt—it will come back to haunt us. Repressing problems invites mental and symptomatic illness to grow from the festering sore of our repressions.

Undoing

The third mechanism people attempt to use when they are at the windowpane of ignoring is undoing.

Years ago, Jimmy Stewart starred in the movie, *It's a Wonderful Life*. He played the part of a manager of a savings and loan company in a small town. One day Jimmy's uncle lost a crucial bank deposit which threatened to break the small savings and loan company. Jimmy Stewart became depressed, walked out on a bridge and contemplated suicide. He cried aloud, "I wish I'd never been born." As the story goes, an angel named Clarence, trying to earn his wings, was sent from God to rescue the despondent man. The angel gave Jimmy Stewart his wish and showed him what the town would have been like if he had never been born. When he realized how many people had been helped through his good deeds, it made him happy to be alive. This is an example of undoing, but notice that it took an angel of God to make it work.

My computer has a command called "undo." Let's say that I am typing along and by accident I press the wrong button and erase the last paragraph I typed. When I press the "undo" button, it cancels the last command. Thus, it brings back my lost paragraph. Don't we all wish we could press the "undo" button in our own lives?

We have probably all thought about "what could have been" if the past could be undone. In reality, though, we can't *undo* the past. The best we can do is to get the past forgiven and remember our mistakes so we don't repeat them.

To accept responsibility for our actions is sometimes a bitter pill to swallow, but if we are to change the future, we must realize that "whatever a man sows, this he will also reap" (Gal. 6:7, NASB).

Recently, I was talking to parents who were having trouble with their teenage son. The mother exclaimed painfully, "What have we done to deserve this?" I knew them when the child was young, and I knew what they had done to deserve their misbehaving son. First, they had not wanted him as a baby. Second, they had neglected him as a child. Third, they paid minimal attention to his accomplishments and maximum attention to his failings. Fourth, they did everything they could to get someone to take the child off their hands. Fifth, they wouldn't pay attention to teachers and experts who told them what the consequences would be of their serious neglect of the child. Now, they can't solve the problem of a rebellious young adult, and they want to practice undoing—they want to pretend that their bad parenting decisions were not made. They just want the problem to go away. They want the schools or God or some agency to perform a miracle and change the problem they created.

If we are going to be problem-solvers, if we are actually going to make anything happen around us, we must look at the problem with all its ugliness, all our contribution, and everything that helped bring the problem to pass. To undo a problem is a fairy story, and those who waste their lives in fairy stories are the most tragic of all people. To accept responsibility for our actions is sometimes a bitter pill to swallow, but if we are to change the future, we must realize that "whatever a man sows, this he will also reap" (Gal. 6:7, NASB).

Once in awhile God in heaven makes a divine intervention on earth just to let us know that He is watching. It is possible for an angel to be sent from heaven to help us. Let's look at a time when that happened and see if they practiced undoing.

Two angels were sent to the ancient cities of Sodom and Gomorrah to warn the residents that the cities would be destroyed if they didn't change their ways. The people didn't change, but those who were receptive to the angels, Lot and his daughters, were led out of the city (Gen. 19). The angels did not automatically make wicked cities righteous. They did not stop the destruction. They merely removed the innocent parties. They didn't *undo* the problem.

I am a perfect example of the futility of the undoing defense mechanism. I have polio. I cannot go back to the age of five and stop the disease from happening. Science cannot heal it, and until God does, what I *can* do is accept my limitations, utilize my virtues, and be as profitable a citizen as those who remain whole. It would be a foolish waste of time to spend my days looking for a way to undo the polio. God wants me to use the polio to give glory to His name. I am to *use* it as a way to solve problems and to inspire others, not to *undo* it.

Summary

Ignoring a problem is a windowpane, and flying that way will never solve anything. If a person continues beating his head against the dead-end street of ignoring, he will end up like the bee, dead on the windowsill of life. By ignoring problems, some people think that they will go away; but what they do is just assume another guise and come at us from another direction. If we do not solve the problem presented to us today, the same problem wearing a mask will approach us tomorrow.

The windowpane of ignoring the problem and its three mechanisms of denial, repression, and undoing do nothing to help us fly free through the open door of a good solution. *What does help is to face our problem.* How to do this is explained in detail in the "Open Doors" section of this book.

Protecting Ourselves from Problems

"The Windowpane of Protecting Ourselves" is the second major reason why people find it difficult to solve problems. People protect themselves from problems as if problems represented hurt, pain, sorrow, death, and the plague.

People often say, "All I want is peace" or "All I want is happiness," but both peace and happiness are results of solving problems. Protecting ourselves does not bring peace or happiness. When Jesus said, "I did not come to bring peace, but a sword" (Matt. 10:34, NASB), He was talking about involvement. To protect ourselves from problems is to protect ourselves from life itself. Unless a person is committed to solving life's problems, he or she will not receive the benefits of life.

There are three methods we use when we are trying to fly through the windowpane of protecting ourselves: defensiveness, rationalization, and avoidance.

Defensiveness

The pain of guilt and the need to avoid disapproval cause us to be very creative in defending ourselves from feelings of responsibility and guilt. When we defend, we do not admit to responsibility or guilt or the truth; rather we consider ourselves under an attack, so we attack back.

To protect ourselves from problems is to protect ourselves from life itself. Unless a person is commited to solving life's problems, he or she will not receive the benefits of life.

A major reason for our existence is to solve problems. That's what most jobs are for—to solve problems. Think for a moment. Without the problem of crime, there would be no police officers, judges, or courts. Without the problem of sickness, there would be no doctors, hospitals, or nurses. In fact, without problems, there would be very little for most people to do. We seldom get paid for recreation, but we do get paid for solving problems. A successful friend of mine has this saying framed on his wall: "The man who has no more problems to solve is out of a job." The person who tries to defend himself against problems is trying to defend himself against life and living.

"Did you make that call to San Francisco?" a coworker asks. "No, I didn't. I'll do it immediately" would be an appropriate problem-solving response. But what does the defensive person do? She proceeds to alleviate guilt by distracting attention away from the problem and creating the diversion of another problem by saying: "I'm doing the best I can—too much is being expected of me," or, "There are only so many hours in the day," or, "Why me? You never pick on anyone else." Our minds are ingenious in defense, but defense is only a distraction from the solution.

One day an argumentative couple came to me for counseling. They specialized in attacking each other and defending themselves. Here is one example of their conversation:

> She attacked, "You never pick up your clothes."
> He defended, "Why should I? I make the money."
> She said, "You are glued to the television set."
> He said, "I'm tired from a hard day's work."
> She, "You never take me anyplace."
> He, "You are always digging in the spurs."
> She, "You have no consideration for me."

In exasperation, I interrupted, "We will get absolutely nowhere in mediating this marriage conflict unless one of you stops defending yourself, admits the other person has made a point, and we try to solve that problem."

Think for a moment. Without the problem of crime, there would be no police officers, judges, or courts. Without the problem of sickness, there would be no doctors, hospitals, or nurses. In fact, without problems, there would be very little for most people to do.

It may be true that a person has a good reason for not solving a problem, but trying to defend him or herself against someone else's confrontation does nothing but delay the solution to the problem.

A wife may say, "Husband, I feel you have become cold and unloving toward me." The husband may reply, "All I get from you is nag, nag, nag. Can't you get off my case?" That answer may be a true expression of the husband's feelings, but it is a defense that leads to no solution. The husband would do far better to stop defending and face the problem of his feelings toward his wife.

It seems as natural as sneezing when we defend ourselves against attack. Like slapping back, defensiveness is a built-in, automatic response to criticism. However, like the windowpane that you can see through but can't get through, defensiveness looks like a way, but it isn't. You can't solve problems when you defend yourself.

When we start to defend ourselves, we basically stop growing. It is almost impossible to heal ourselves of any bad habit unless we first admit the bad habit exists.

I have had years of experience in dealing with alcoholics, and I have a clear-cut rule based on my experience. I will not counsel a man or woman who is drinking. But I will talk all night to a sober person who tells me, "I am an alcoholic and I want to drink. Help me stop." Until the addicted person admits he or she has the problem and stops defending, there is no answer.

When someone has said something untrue, or partially true, or taken out of context, or wrongly interpreted, it is okay to defend yourself. However, sometimes the best defense against a lie is silence. We are talking about those people who never admit to even obvious truth, and so do not solve the problems of life.

Rationalization

Protecting ourselves from the problem takes on another dimension in the defense mechanism of rationalization. Rationalization is the fine art of excuse-making.

On occasion, there are some good reasons for failure to solve problems. A few problems are unsolvable, but not as many as the person who rationalizes would have us think.

Problems seem to cluster together, organize, and attack a person. To make excuses delays the inevitable for only a short time. Let's say you have some work to do. Work is merely unsolved problems. Roll up your sleeves and get the work done before it gets you done. Making up reasons for not doing the work only delays the solution to the problem.

The number one rationalization is "I forgot." It's the first rationalization children learn. You tell them to pick up their clothes. They respond by protecting themselves, saying: "I forgot."

To say, "I forgot" means that you have become so practiced and skilled in avoiding responsibility that you have your unconscious mind hooked into making you forget so that you don't have to face the problem.

A man came to see me with a problem. He was very sarcastic. His wife said she could no longer tolerate his biting words. I thought it was of the utmost importance for the man to say something nice to his wife when she walked into the room. So, I briefed him to say, "Honey, that's a pretty dress." When she walked into the room, he put heavy emphasis on the word *that's* and said sarcastically, "*That's* a pretty dress?" His wife promptly stomped out.

"I thought you were going to say something nice!" I said.

He muttered, "I forgot."

The word *excuse* is in the English vocabulary, but it is used too often. It won't work; it's a windowpane.

When I was a psychologist at Terminal Island Federal Penitentiary in California, I discovered that some of the convicts had raised rationalization to such a fine art that it was easy for them to believe that wrong was right and night was day. Rationalizers can often intellectualize themselves into any position.

A thief once said to me, "Why do people pick on me? I'm the most valuable man in the community. I steal from people, and they collect more than the item is worth from the insurance company. The police are called and it gives them something to do. The neighborhood is in an uproar and they receive lots of excitement and pleasure from all the gossip. I make a little money to stay alive and so does the pawnbroker. Look at all the people I put to work." The thief had constructed this elaborate rationalization to justify stealing.

In listening to the tapes from the Watergate scandal, the news reported Richard Nixon to have said, "Well, one thing for sure, it would be wrong." If that thoughtful statement had turned him around, we would not have had the Watergate scandal and history would be different. One thing is sure: it was wrong to go that way, but after hours of intellectualization, misconstrued semantics and mind-changing rationalization, that which is wrong can appear to be right. We can justify almost anything if we are clever with the use of words.

We can justify almost anything if we are clever with the use of words.

Rather than rationalization, why not try honesty?

"Yes, I am an alcoholic." Now you can work on it.

"Yes, I am too extravagant." Now you can change.

"Yes, I am short-tempered." Now you can work on becoming a more controlled person.

"Yes, I have trouble saying *no* when someone asks me to do something." Now we can find out why and get to work solving the problem.

"Yes, I am late. I did not get up on time." Now you can work on the problem of lateness.

A young lady who was working as a cook in the army came in for counseling. Every morning she was expected to arrive at 6:00. If she was late by even one minute, she had to do a double shift. This nineteen-year-old girl had been doing a double shift every day for nine months. She spoke of the cruelty of the United States Army, the meanness of the captain in charge, the loss of her health, etc.

I asked her, "Why didn't you come to work on time?"
"I just couldn't, and they knew I couldn't, and they took advantage of me," she said.

A perfect rationalization. The real problem was not the cruelty of the army but the inability of the young lady to face her problem of lateness. She defended herself against the problem until she became mentally ill and broken.

Avoidance

Another technique people use to protect themselves against problems and problem-solving is called avoidance. To put off solving a problem by avoiding doesn't do one thing toward changing things.

One of the great stories of all time is the story of the good Samaritan. A man was going from Jerusalem to Jericho when he fell among thieves who robbed him, beat him, and left him lying stripped and unconscious beside the road. A priest was going along the same road. He saw the man and thought to himself, *If I had more time, I would help him, but I must get to the conference,* so he avoided the man and went on his way. Then a temple teacher came by and made the same excuses. Finally, a hated Samaritan stopped and helped the wounded man and took him to an inn to recuperate (Luke 10:29–37). Today the story of the good Samaritan has become symbolic of man's brotherhood to man, of practicing the Golden Rule, and accepting responsibility rather than protecting oneself.

All history rises up and reveres this person who faced his problems, saw his responsibility, and did the task that was presented to him. The word *Samaritan* was a hated word preceded by a sneer. It has now become one of literature's greatest symbols because one man saw a problem and accepted his responsibility. He did not practice avoidance.

One of the major thrusts of psychology tells us how devastating a defense mechanism can be. Avoidance of our problems only leads to personal destruction. The rule is: When you have a problem, admit it quickly and emphatically. Face it bravely with resolution. Look it over fearlessly. Describe it accurately. Consider solutions and alternatives. Choose a solution and act upon it. To deny a problem's existence or to defend ourselves against its solution is as fruitless as the bee beating its wings against the windowpane. It won't work, and it never will.

Recently, a couple came to see me. The woman had a long list of grievances against her husband, and he had a long list against her. Everything they had written seemed so trivial to me. I asked them, "What happens when you discuss these things with each other?" They both responded, "We never discuss our problems with each other. We avoid them so we can have a happy marriage."

"Do you have a happy marriage?"

They both replied, "No."

"How do you feel toward each other?"

"We hate each other."

"Why have you come to me?" I asked.

"Perhaps if we face our problems and stop avoiding discussions, we will learn how to solve our problems and no longer hate each other."

Maybe that's why the couple was so easy to counsel and bring back to the state of love. They could quickly admit that they were not facing their problems.

To defend ourselves by rationalization or by simple avoidance makes the predictions of psychology come true: we will be filled with guilt and anxiety and lose our joy of living.

I have used many defense mechanisms, and I've heard many more. If you like ways of protecting yourself from solving problems, here are a few that you may add to your repertoire:

"I didn't feel like it."	Defensiveness
"I was too tired."	Defensiveness
"I'm going to do it tomorrow."	Avoidance
"My tools broke."	Rationalization
"The weather was too bad."	Defensiveness
"It's a holiday."	Rationalization
"Some relatives came to visit."	Defensiveness
"My husband/wife wouldn't let me."	Avoidance
"I had better things to do."	Rationalization
"The problem will wait."	Avoidance
"It's too late to do it now."	Avoidance
"I'm not strong enough."	Defensiveness
"I'm not big enough."	Defensiveness
"I'm not well enough."	Defensiveness
"I'm not smart enough."	Defensiveness
"I'm not getting paid enough."	Rationalization
"Someone else will do it."	Avoidance
"Why me? I solved the last problem."	Defensiveness
"It isn't fair."	Rationalization
"I'm the only one with problems."	Defensiveness

You may ask how I know so much about excuse-making. I shudder to admit that I am a master excuse-maker myself. But I am living proof that an ace "defender" can really change. (Well, at least I'm getting better.)

Summary

The three ways our personality handles the windowpane of protecting ourselves from problems are: defensiveness, protecting ourselves against the demands of the problem; rationalization, making reasonable sounding excuses for not doing a task; and avoidance, putting it off until another time.

None of these mechanisms work. So why not make a mental decision to get on with your life and tackle without hesitation the next problem that comes along?

Retreating
from Problems

"The Windowpane of Retreating from Problems" is a real
dead-end street. Instead of denying the problem exists or
protecting ourselves, we retreat into the rosy glow of non-
reality.

The windowpane of retreating has three defense mechanisms, or three ways of reacting: fantasy, regression, and
disassociation.

Fantasy

Fantasy is dreaming about something else instead of
facing the problem. I love the windowpane of retreating
into fantasy. It has such a rosy glow. I have often beat my
wings against its attractive panes. But even when I have
fallen faint in the gutter of the window, there seems to be
a special pleasure in trying to solve my problems through

fantasy. When the bully of life kicks sand in my face and challenges me, I dream glorious dreams of becoming the strongest man in the world, of beating up that terrible bully and winning the hand of the fair maiden.

Ah, fantasy! To fly faster than a speeding bullet; to have the wisdom of an army of think tankers; to sit in the mythical car of my daydreams and parade down the streets of life as the people shower me with confetti and ticker tape. I love fantasy, but no matter how attractively the rose-tinted window of fantasy glows, you can't solve your problems that way.

I love fantasy, but no matter how attractively the rose-tinted window of fantasy glows, you can't solve your problems that way.

About five years ago Jackie came to see me. She was so disappointed with her life. She said, "I am on welfare; I haven't finished high school; I can't find a job; I need plastic surgery after an automobile accident; I feel like life has passed me by." I encouraged Jackie to go back to school and to learn a trade.

Recently Jackie came in again. She said, "I am exactly where I was five years ago when I first met you. I am still on welfare; I haven't finished high school; I can't find a job; and I still need plastic surgery. Life is still passing me by."

I said to her, "Jackie, why do you suppose this is happening to you?"

She replied, "I suppose I get so much pleasure out of dreaming about success that I never get around to doing anything about it."

Jackie has substituted fantasy for problem-solving. If she continues, five years or fifty will pass by and she will be where she is now.

We can daydream our lives away and never solve a single problem. Of course, there is constructive fantasy such as creative dreaming, brainstorming, and considering far-fetched solutions and fantastic alternatives. Those are okay. Imagination is good, but fantasy is an escape mechanism that won't work.

Fantasy also has some inherent dangers. One of the chief dangers of fantasy is that awful word *schizophrenia*.

We can daydream our lives away and never solve a single problem.

A schizophrenic is one who escapes from the reality of life by internalizing the world. The schizophrenic solves problems that do not exist in a world that is not there. A schizophrenic cannot cope with the frustrations that life puts upon her. So she lives in a dream world where she can make her own problems, and create her own solutions with dynamics that won't work any place but fantasyland.

In fantasyland you do not have to pay attention to the laws of nature or the laws of cause and effect or the laws of science. The great discoveries from physics and chemistry that tell us how things really are have no validity in the world of fantasy. In fantasy, things are not as they are; they are any way we choose them to be. If we are on the top of a tall building, in reality, we must come down by the stairs or the elevator. In fantasy, we suddenly find ourselves at the bottom.

Too many people get themselves painted into a corner by the brush strokes of their inventions. There is no solution to their dilemma; they are trapped. So they try to solve their problems via fantasy—trying to do something that in real life they cannot do.

Flexibility and imagination are often an answer to the dilemma of being trapped in a corner. To be flexible, to be willing to consider another way and to be imaginative, to think of alternatives are solutions discussed in the "Open Door" chapters. Flexibility and imagination are not fantasy. The real world offers flexibility and creative imagination and sometimes we can wiggle our way out of the corner like a fish wiggles away from a shark.

When you solve your problems with faith and reality, you don't need to escape into the world of fantasy.

Fantasy demands a miracle when flexibility and imagination could more easily solve the problem. Fantasy often senselessly martyrs itself and dies for causes that do not exist. Fantasy often screams its madness to the ears of sane people, demanding that they do something about a world that isn't there.

Fantasy has nothing to do with faith. Faith believes in reality. Faith believes that the Creator did a good job. Faith has tremendous power because it sides with reality until it can literally take mountains and cast them into the sea. The person who cooperates with the way things work has the power of the universe on his side.

I'll never forget Melvin because he was such a prime example of fantasy. He did not bother with schizoid fantasy which allows the mind to drift off into an irresponsible world of its own. He used TV fantasy. He allowed television programs to mesmerize him. Melvin lay immobile in his bed, totally immersed in whatever drama television brewed. Melvin sold real estate, that is, when he got out of bed. The problem is that selling real estate, like selling anything, requires consistency, hard work, and dedicated enthusiasm. Melvin could not measure up, so he lay down and dreamed.

I suggested to Melvin that his mountainous problems were merely molehills that could easily be climbed if he faced them one at a time. "That's easier said than done," reasoned Melvin. Fortunately, I persuaded him that it could be done and that the worst thing he could do was to lay in bed and let TV be his reality.

Falseness lives in the world of fantasy. Truth lives in the world of reality. Faith makes reality work. Fantasy, our response to frustration, will not solve life's problems. Chapter 7, "Defining," tells how to look at problems realistically with faith. When you solve your problems with faith and reality, you don't need to escape into the world of fantasy.

Regression

Regression is retreating to an earlier maturity level or acting like a baby. Sometimes, it's reverting to childlike techniques: lying on the floor, kicking and screaming when you don't get your way. It's expressing emotional frustration at the problem in hopes that someone else will run to you and say, "Poor baby, let me do it for you."

Asking someone to help you solve your problem is an honest, straightforward technique for solving some of the most formidable problems of life. But manipulating people and getting them to do your will by an emotional tirade only makes them feel used and angry. And guess who eventually pays the bill for that?

Not long ago I treated a forty-year-old man who was having trouble with his marriage. Ben seemed unable to do the simplest tasks to assist his wife around the house. He would not take out the garbage, mow the lawn, pick up his clothes, or have proper table manners. His wife nagged him as if he were a young boy. One day I asked him, "How old are you, Ben?"

"Nine, going on forty."

"What do you mean by that?"

"I am forty, but I feel like I am nine."

I said to him, "If you can't grow up and act like a man, how do you expect your wife to remain married to a nine-year-old?"

"That's a good question," he responded, "and I suppose you're going to tell me that the reason I can't hold down a job is because I am acting like a child."

"You said it."

I wish this story had a happy ending, but Ben never chose to grow up and act like a man. He faced the problems of life with the emotional strength of a nine-year-old. His habit of regressing to an earlier maturity level did not give him enough strength to solve adult problems.

Regression is expressing emotional frustration at the problem in hopes that someone else will run to you and say, "Poor baby, let me do it for you."

Today, psychology has a new term, EDS, or Emotional Dysfunction Syndrome. I actually have clients whose only excuse for their regressive childlike behavior is to claim lamely, "I have EDS."

Sometimes when people do not know how to solve their problems, they regress to a helpless baby attitude, hoping that someone else will solve the problem for them. One day I said to a healthy young man, "If you expended as much effort in getting and holding a job as you do in persuading our government to take care of you, you surely would be rich and successful."

Regression does succeed occasionally, but so does robbing banks at gunpoint. Solving the problems of life by regressing does not work consistently. In fact, just the opposite is true. Most of the time, we solve problems by

1. acting like an adult,
2. learning from our mistakes,
3. correcting our errors,
4. growing up, and
5. intelligently choosing alternative roads when the road we are following leads to a windowpane.

When we were children, we had parents who were responsible for our lives. We learned as babies that when we cried, our parents came and took away the frustrating thing that was bothering us. They solved our problems and dried our tears.

There are some adults that continue to get their way by crying or stomping their feet or pouting until they win the confrontation. The sad thing is, if they win, they really lose. They lose out on the joys of positive, equal, face-to-face relationships. People dread being around a regressive personality. They know they have to weigh carefully every word to keep from hurting his feelings and give in to his desires to keep him from making a scene. If he only knew how many fine friendships and experiences of life he was missing.

Recently, a woman said to me, "I am so tired of walking on eggshells. My husband is so sensitive that I never know when I am going to use a word or turn a phrase that will cause an angry reaction. He wears his feelings on his sleeve and dares anyone to touch him. He is such a baby; I don't think I can love him much longer."

I suppose everyone can remember a person whose sensitivities were so childlike that we could not relate to him or her. Certainly it is not possible for a person who is acting like a child to solve the problems of the adult world.

Dr. Eric Berne, famous author and developer of Transactional Analysis, divides our responses into three categories which he calls parent, adult, and child. All three responses are healthy and normal. But when one position becomes too dominant, we appear unbalanced. He says, "The child in us is that charming, 'help me please' and 'see what I can do' state that is important in adding that extra sizzle to marriage and friendship. Our inner child personality makes life fun. We should never allow our child to die; it should simply be tempered with the parent and the adult that lives inside us too."

It's fun to watch adults play. I watched a couple at the Long Beach Civic Opera one evening. Instead of standing sedately beside his wife on the outdoor escalator, this young man chose to slide down the escalator handrail, arms and feet flapping with meticulous ease. The "see what I can do" twinkle in his eye warmed everyone's heart. It was refreshing to see two people so accepting of each other's "child" at play. In facing the grimness of life, it helps to maintain the childlike spirit of fun.

However, when a person allows the child in him to grow too big and acts childish too much of the time, he has trouble. The adult who regresses to child-like irresponsibility is a person who can't solve problems.

Paul the apostle said, "When I was a child, I talked like a child, I thought like a child, I reasoned like a child. When I became a man, I put childish ways behind me" (1 Cor. 13:11, NIV). We too need to remember that as adults, it doesn't work to go back to our childish ways of solving problems. As adults, we meet the challenges of life like adults. We (1) learn from our mistakes, (2) correct our errors, (3) intelligently *choose* alternative roads when we are blocked, (4) don't allow our emotionality to manipulate others into surrendering for "peace at any price," and (5) are optimistic about the future and press on toward the high goals we have determined for ourselves. To go back to childhood does not solve problems. To go forward and grow into maturity is a step in the right direction. Regression is a windowpane. Progression is an open door.

Disassociation

Disassociation is removing ourselves from the problem as if it didn't belong to us.

Disassociation sidesteps the problem, saying foolishly, "It's not my responsibility to take care of my teeth."

Matthew 27:22–24 (NIV) tells us that when Jesus was brought to Pilate for judgment, Pilate made an attempt to free him. But the crowd loudly cried for Barabbas. Pilate asked, "What shall I do, then, with Jesus who is called Christ?" The crowd screamed, "Crucify him!" When Pilate saw that he was getting nowhere and that an uproar was starting, he took water and washed his hands in front of the crowd. "I am innocent of this man's blood," he said. "It is your responsibility!" Pilate didn't know it, but he was guilty of disassociation. It was his responsibility to judge Jesus. He disassociated himself from the problem and allowed the crowd to have its way. So the greatest crime of history was perpetrated.

Defending yourself at least admits that the problem is your business. To repress a problem means to gather it to your bosom and bury it in your memory, thinking if you can't remember it, it will go away. It's like subconsciously forgetting a dental appointment—the cavity is still there. However, disassociation sidesteps the problem, saying foolishly, "It's not my responsibility to take care of my teeth."

When there is a crime wave in the community and a person says, "It's not my problem," she is guilty of disassociation. People sometimes think they don't have to solve the problem when they say, "It's not my problem."

The problem with disassociation is that when we remove ourselves from problems, we also remove ourselves from blessings. If we can't face hate, we won't get love. If we can't face fear, we will never have faith. If we can't face hopelessness, we will never experience hope. To disassociate ourselves from problems is to disassociate ourselves from growth and blessing.

A few years ago on the city streets of New York, Kitty Genovese came to international attention. She was stabbed to death on her own doorstep in full view of thirty other people in her apartment complex who admitted seeing the act. Sociologists are still investigating the phenomenon. The people disassociated themselves from the problem, thinking that someone else would call the police or act responsibly. We have no way of knowing how many Kitty Genoveses have died because of the defense mechanism of disassociation.

In the Bible, at the beginning of the human race, Cain murdered his brother Abel. When God called him to account, Cain disassociated with the words, "Am I my brother's keeper?" (Gen. 4:9, NIV). The story of God's intervention with man has answered this question a thousand times. Yes, you are your brother's keeper. Don't disassociate. It is your problem.

Summary

We have learned that we don't solve problems by persisting at the windowpanes of ignoring, protecting, or retreating.

The windowpane of retreating has three ways it manifests itself in life:

1. Fantasy: daydreaming about something else.

2. Regression: manipulating others into solving our problems for us by acting like a baby.
3. Disassociation: removing ourselves from the problem as if it didn't belong to us.

We don't solve problems by retreating into any of the above avenues. When we realize we are retreating as we face the daily problems of life, then we know it is time to turn around and look for open doors.

Blaming

"The Windowpane of Blaming" attacks everything but the problem. We attack the circumstances, other people, or sometimes even God. To blame is to distract from coming to a solution. If we attack the problem without placing blame, we have a problem-solving mechanism. But to blame is to futilely attack anything except the problem.

There are three mechanisms or ways of blaming: introjection, projection, and displacement.

Introjection

Introjection is blaming yourself for the problem, perhaps even engaging in self-punishing techniques. This dichotomous windowpane is similar to glass that is painted silver on one side. You look into the window and you see the reflection of yourself. You look at the problem, and in all honesty, you can see that *you* are the one who caused the problem. The dichotomy is that the more you blame yourself for causing the problem, the less likely you are to find a solution.

It is one thing to accept responsibility, and it's another thing to blame ourselves and involve ourselves in incrimination and self-punishment techniques. Guilt is a terrible vengeance taker, and self-punishment is actually a distraction from the solution. If we are going to solve the problem, it makes very little difference who is to blame for it. So, if it's your fault, spend your time on making a plan to correct the error and solve the problem. Incrimination is a waste of time. It's a windowpane.

The more you blame yourself for causing the problem, the less likely you are to find a solution.

Some people are their own worst enemies. Recently a lady came to me for counseling. She said, "In a court battle with my husband, I told the court psychologist that my husband claimed, 'She is a prostitute. She is crazy, and she is not a fit mother for the children.' When the court psychologist made his report to the judge, he repeated those ideas to the court. Somehow there was a subtle implication that I was a prostitute, that I was crazy, and that I was an unfit mother. None of those charges are true."

The woman had felt constrained to tell the psychologist and the judge what her husband said about her. Thus, she became her husband's gossip, her own slanderer, and her own worst enemy.

Don't repeat the bad things people say about you. Repeat the good things. Don't advertise your enemy; advertise your friend. If everyone in the group rises up and says, "It's your fault," then reply, "So what? Let's do something about it."

Introjection, or blaming yourself, is very different from honestly confessing your faults or from accepting responsibility for misdeeds. Blaming includes punishment. Introjection implies a way to concentrate upon yourself. It is a subtle way of being self-centered. To say, "Yes, I did wrong," to ask God to forgive you, to be sorry, to make restitution if possible, to repent, and not to do it again are all fine helps. But to continue to blame yourself puts negative attention on you and sometimes becomes so satisfying and attention-getting that it turns to masochism. Then a person spends his lifetime trying to find ways to punish himself. Don't waste time blaming yourself. Solve the problem if you can. If not, accept the idea that you did the best you could.

Don't repeat the bad things people say about you. Repeat the good things.

When I worked as a consulting psychologist in the prison system, I discovered that some prisoners become very negative about themselves and begin to blame themselves for everything. It was common to hear these words from an inmate, "Well, I really didn't do the crime I was sentenced for, but I did so many other things, I guess I richly deserve this punishment. So, I just accept it." That's called introjection.

Have you ever taken the blame, even when you didn't do the deed, because of how you felt about yourself? One needs to be extremely careful when he gets to that point because suicide is the ultimate introjection.

King Saul was very jealous of David. When coming back from a war, the maidens sang, "Saul has slain his thousands, and David his ten thousands" (1 Sam. 29:5, NASB). So, Saul shortly formed a plan to kill David. One day David caught Saul asleep in a cave and he could have easily killed him, but David did not. When David's action was revealed to Saul, Saul cried and said to David, "You are more righteous than I; for you have dealt well with me, while I have dealt wickedly with you" (1 Sam. 24:17, NASB). Saul did not work on his problem of jealousy; he merely confessed that it was his fault. Because he did not solve this problem, he pursued David to the end of his days, and the kingdom was lost to him. Saul is a perfect example of introjection—blaming himself but not solving the problem.

Saul could have taken David back as one of his captains, accepted the plan of God that David was to be the next king, and groomed David for the task. If Saul had confessed his jealousy instead of his guilt and solved his problem instead of blaming himself, the name of King Saul would now be reverenced along with King David. Introjection, blaming oneself, only makes the problem worse. Solving the problem is the theme of this book.

We live in a country that practices democracy, but under certain circumstances, we allow totalitarian dictatorships to exist. One of those circumstances is aboard a sea-going vessel. The captain is absolute dictator of his ship. But with this glorious privilege goes an ominous responsibility. If something happens to the ship, it's the captain's fault. That's why some captains go down with the ship. Similarly, we often go down with our "ship" when the establishing of blame becomes the only criterion of leadership.

During World War II, Admiral Bull Halsey dismissed the captain of a carrier because one of the elevators in the carrier broke. An aide to Admiral Halsey said, "But sir, it wasn't the captain's fault the elevator broke. He was just unlucky." The admiral replied, "I don't want unlucky captains manning my fleet. Transfer him."

That's the result of absolute responsibility and absolute blame. Life can be unfair enough. We don't need to add to its problems. Placing blame on ourselves will not solve a problem. It will only get us dismissed.

Placing blame on ourselves will not solve a problem. It will only get us dismissed.

Projection

In projection we blame others and often attack them instead of solving problems.

Everything said about introjection—blaming ourselves—is doubly true about *projection*—blaming other people. Both introjection and projection are distractions that look like a way out but actually keep us from solving the problem.

Projection is an interesting concept. In a movie theater, the celluloid film that contains the action for the movie runs through a projector, but the picture via light and mirrors is projected onto a screen. The real picture is in the machine, but the machine's purpose is to send the picture from itself to another place. That's the problem with projection. Often, the real problem, the action itself is in the person, but the person is projecting the problem out there as if everyone else is to blame.

Sometimes people *are* to blame, but my point in both introjection and projection is that blame does not solve the problem any more than diagnosis provides the cure for an illness. Many people content themselves with diagnosis, name-calling, and blame-fixing and never realize that those things don't change the nature of the problem.

An example of this is the common American practice of blaming the president of the United States for our economic problems. If we are going to solve the problems of our nation, we need to do more than blame one man. We all can share in some responsibility for economic problems.

Blame does not solve the problem any more than diagnosis provides the cure for an illness. Many people content themselves with diagnosis, name-calling, and blame-fixing and never realize that those things don't change the nature of the problem.

I recall counseling a heroin addict. With the zeal of a crusader, I rolled up my sleeves to help this young man. His parents were devastated by his habit. I soon discovered why it is so difficult to cure narcotic addiction. Not only is there a physical dependency; there is also a psychological dependency. Often, the user develops a "line" like my young client. He flopped himself down in my overstuffed chair, looked me in the eye and said, "I'm in your hands. Do with me what you will. But first, I need to tell you my problem—I've run out of heroin. I'm having a spasm, and I've got to get a fix or I won't even be able to live." He tried to hook me into providing him with drugs out of human sympathy for his suffering. When I refused he said, "Well, here I thought you psychologists cared about people's suffering. You really proved to me that you don't care. All you want is your fee." Somehow, his heroin addiction became all *my* fault. Thus, he didn't have to solve the problem because it wasn't *his* problem.

We have all experienced the game of blaming others. It's a favorite trick of small children. As adults, it's easy to get caught up in blaming our parents for our own emotional problems, blaming our schoolteachers for our lack of knowledge, blaming our politicians for the lack of jobs, blaming our doctors for our poor health.

A lady dying of cancer came to see me. She had been so careful to go to the doctor as soon as she noticed the lump in her breast. She was bitter because she had done everything she could to get well but it wasn't working. Judy angrily said, "Our society has the technology to put someone on the moon, but no technology to save me from cancer." During our interview, I learned she had dissipated most of her life with alcohol binges and four packs of cigarettes a day. She now wanted to blame everyone for her physical problem—everyone but herself. Blaming herself would not cure the cancer, but neither would blaming the medical doctors.

Blame doesn't solve problems. No matter how noble it sounds to say, "I have no one to blame but myself," that statement does not change anything. No matter how cruelly we are treated by others, in the final analysis it does no good to blame someone else for our problems.

I will never forget the tears and pain of a thirty-year-old woman who told me of the emotional upset in her life because of molestation as a child. I had great sympathy for her. I believe her nervous breakdown at thirty could be traced directly to her terrible childhood experiences. I put a lot of effort into helping her heal those bad memories. I even found the relative who was responsible and arranged a meeting. He asked forgiveness. But in the final analysis, she had to solve the problem based on the present. All her blaming of others, her projection of the problem, her finding the causes were helpful, but they ended up not being the solution.

Eventually, problems must be squarely faced. Finding out who caused the problem and blaming them is really a distraction. It is a windowpane, not a solution.

Finding out who caused the problem and blaming them is really a distraction. It is a windowpane, not a solution.

Displacement

Displacement is the third way of operating the windowpane of blaming. We blame some element connected to the problem instead of using our energy to solve it.

Instead of facing the problem, many immature adults get mad at it. They direct their anger at the problem and ignore the solution. If the car won't start, they kick it. Anger moves everyone out of the way; but after the anger, the problem still exists. Getting angry at a problem won't solve it any more than kicking a tire will start a car.

I'll never forget how awed I was the day my father stepped on the prongs of the garden rake. The handle came up and hit him on the forehead. He took the rake and beat it to death against the side of the garage. The result: a mutilated rake, repairs to the garage, and a trip to the doctor for medicine for Dad's stomach ulcer. Displacement— becoming angry at the problem—leaves the problem intact, as my father discovered.

Anger is like a bottle of nitroglycerin; it can go off unexpectedly. To have misdirected anger means to clasp to your bosom a hot bottle of nitroglycerin. The problems of life are not getting solved; we just hurt ourselves or someone else. A policeman friend of mine tells me that over half of the homicides in our country are done under the influence of impulsive, destructive anger. Few people deliberately sit down and plan to harm someone. Boom! It just happens. However, to become frustrated at a problem and impulsively smash anyone identified with the problem will not solve it.

A bruised and battered young lady came into my office. One eye was swollen shut, bruises were prominent on her face, neck, and arms. Her demeanor was one of despair. Her boyfriend had become angry at her for allegedly flirting with another man. After hearing her story and giving her proper solace for the bruising, I became convinced that she was indeed an outrageous flirt. That was the problem. But the solution to the problem was not displacement—beating up the flirt. The boyfriend's method did not solve the problem of her flirtatious ways, and neither did his method keep his girlfriend. Furthermore, the method of displacement can be criminal, dangerous and counterproductive.

Displacement is deceptive in that we often feel highly motivated when we are angry, but to kick the car when it won't go and to hit our girlfriend when she is flirtatious will not create the desired changes.

Anger directed at the problem is destructive. Anger directed toward a *solution* can be problem-solving. Displacement is deceptive in that we often feel highly motivated when we are angry, but to kick the car when it won't go and to hit our girlfriend when she is flirtatious will not create the desired changes.

Displacement blindly attacks the air. We may create a tiny wind or stir up a few dust particles, but we will not solve the problem. Problems are solved by action, not reaction.

Recently a man with an emotional dysfunction syndrome came to me for treatment. I asked his wife, "What does your husband do when he gets angry?" She responded, "Oh, sometimes he puts his fist through a door and sometimes he tears it down. When he gets frustrated, nothing is safe within his reach." Anyone can see the futility of building up a furnace of fire not to heat the building but to burn it down.

It is actually much easier to solve problems than to bear the consequences of an emotional discharge that fruitlessly fires the air. Such needless discharge of our emergency alarm system creates a stress that is cumulative. The constant firing of the electrical chemical system that runs our body eventually breaks down the system. Not only does a person fail to solve his problems with displacement, but he eventually has the most severe problem of all—a physiological illness that defies medical solution. Those people who face a problem by displacing their anger onto another person or object often find that they have not vented their rage but rather made it worse. Perhaps running around the block will reduce anger at a problem, but pulling up people's flowers on the way around the block will exacerbate anger and worsen the problem.

Displacement makes people ill. The young man who battered his girlfriend for flirting soon found that his method of displacement gave him a bout with the police and stomach ulcers. The rage my father indulged in made him sick. Displacing his anger sent him on an endless search for solutions to his ulcers, psoriasis, high blood pressure, and various other physical ailments. All my father needed to do was to direct his energy toward solving the problem, not toward beating the problem to death. Pick up the rake, Daddy, and put it away. It will save a trip to the health resort sitting in mudpacks and mineral baths seeking to cure problems that were caused by simple displacement.

Sigmund Freud invented the term *hysteria* from the Greek word meaning "womb." He thought it was a women's disease. But hysteria belongs to both men and women. It means manipulating people through immature emotional reactions.

I remember treating a woman who faced the problem of remodeling her house by screaming at her husband when he didn't properly install a kitchen sink. After a screaming rage, she went into a three-week period of silence. The displacement cost her a husband, a home, and a house that never did get remodeled.

I remember treating a woman who faced the problem of remodeling her house by screaming at her husband when he didn't properly install a kitchen sink. After a screaming rage, she went into a three-week period of silence. The displacement cost her a husband, a home, and a house that never did get remodeled.

Of all the things that people do to avoid accepting responsibility for the problems life hands them, an emotional displacement is among the most futile. If a man chooses to lie on the ground and kick and scream or to sulk and act like a baby, he will soon find all he gets is a trip to the hospital with a nervous breakdown.

Chapter 12, "Motivating," will teach you how to direct your emotions instead of resorting to the defense mechanism of displacement.

The poem "Opportunity" graphically illustrates displacement.

> This I beheld, or dreamed it in a dream:—
> There spread a cloud of dust across a plain;
> And underneath the cloud, or in it, raged
> A furious battle, and men yelled, and swords
> Shocked upon swords and shields. A prince's banner
> Wavered, then staggered backward, hemmed by foes.
> A craven hung along the battle's edge,
> And thought, 'Had I a sword of keener steel—
> That blue blade that the king's son bears,— but this
> Blunt thing!' he snapped and flung it from his hand,
> And lowering, crept away and left the field.
> Then came the king's son, wounded, sore bestead,
> And weaponless, and saw the broken sword,
> Hilt buried in the dry and trodden sand,
> And ran and snatched it, and with battle shout
> Lifted afresh, he hewed his enemy down,
> And saved a great cause that heroic day.

—Edward Roland Sill, 1841–1887

The craven solved the problem of fighting by displacing his energy onto his sword. He broke his sword, which then gave him the excuse *not* to fight the battle he had been assigned. The king's son was not looking for an excuse, nor did he displace his energy onto any object. The king's son found in a broken sword an opportunity. All problem-solvers are kings' sons. Those who displace must claim the name "Craven."

Summary

Looking through the windowpane of blaming, we see lots of wasted energy that could have been used to solve the problem.

The three mechanisms of blaming—introjection, projection, and displacement—only distract our attention from finding a solution. In introjection, we blame ourselves; in projection, we blame someone else; and in displacement, we blame circumstances. But, in any of the three, we don't use our energy to solve the problem. The vigor of the attack may make it seem like an open door, but in reality, to put energy into anything except the solution is a windowpane.

Negative Transfer

"The Windowpane of Negative Transfer" is a dangerous method of avoiding problem-solving by using converting disorder, negativism, or reaction formation. Those people who engage in changing the problem into something worse suffer from consequences that range from physical illness to emotional illness through mental illness to actual death.

Converting Disorder

The first method of negative transfer is a defense mechanism called converting disorder. For example, instead of solving the problem, we get sick, and then we don't have to solve it.

When I was a schoolboy, the teacher announced we were going to have a test at the end of the week. Instead of studying for the test, I played. Friday morning came too swiftly. As I prepared to go to school, I knew I could not pass that test. I became so worried and anxious that I appeared at the breakfast table with a pained look on my face. My mother asked me, "What's wrong, son?"

Instead of saying, "I'm worried about a test we're having today in math," I said, "I don't feel well."

"Where do you hurt?"

"All over. I have a terrible stomachache. I can't eat breakfast."

Mother put me to bed and properly babied me. I got out of taking the test. I converted my problem into a sickness and temporarily avoided it. That's called solving your problems through a converting disorder.

Converting your problems into a sickness sometimes allows you to avoid the problem temporarily, but changing your problem into a physical complaint will not and cannot solve the problem.

You might ask, "But it works sometimes, doesn't it?" The answer is, "No." Converting your problems into a sickness sometimes allows you to avoid the problem *temporarily,* but changing your problem into a physical complaint will not and cannot solve the problem.

A psychosomatic illness is a self-generated illness—a breakdown in which a person actually makes himself or herself sick, usually without being aware that he or she is doing it. Instead of a germ, bacteria, virus or trauma causing the hurt, we unconsciously make ourselves sick through mind power, desire, or secret control of the autonomic nervous system or the endocrine glands. The human being has the power, with practice, to cause the white cells to lie down on the job and not obey their natural instinct to fight the invaders.

So many illnesses are of a psychogenic nature. They are caused by the psychology of the person. If we have a massive bacterial invasion so that the immune system is overwhelmed, we will get an illness; but if the immune system refuses to fight, even a small army of invaders can make the body sick.

So, it really doesn't make much difference whether the bacteria are too strong or the immune system is too weak; the person will have the same illness.

The worst fool of all is the fool who tries to fool himself.

There are some people who become extremely skillful at the converting disorder. They learn how to persuade the white cells not to fight back. Therefore, they get benefits from getting sick. Poor sick dear! No one's going to expect him or her to work or face problems or do the job or assume responsibilities or overcome frustrations or "fight the good fight of life." He or she is sick, really sick, not just pretending. So he or she doesn't have to go to that job or cope with those kids or go to war.

The child who avoids taking the test by feigning sickness is conscious of his plan, but with the psychosomatic illness, it is an unconscious process. He or she gets sick by powerful subconscious control of the immune or autonomic nervous system.

I'm not saying that everyone who gets sick is subconsciously causing the sickness. There are people who get genuine illnesses. But there are also people whose illness is generated by their own clever secret techniques of manipulating the autonomic nervous system.

How do we tell the difference? The answer to that is not easy. And there isn't a doctor around who hasn't been fooled by psychosomatic illnesses. However, the worst fool of all is the fool who tries to fool himself. Perhaps secretly, you are the only one who will know when you "play the converting game" to keep from facing a problem. Being honest with ourselves is often most painful.

Here's an idea to remember: always consider the possibility that you may be contributing to your own illness. By all means, use the expertise of the medical authorities, but equally, *assume responsibility*, cooperate with the doctor, and *think* of yourself as feeling well.

As Christians, we assume responsibility for our wellness by getting proper rest, exercise, and food, but we also lean on Jesus for his healing touch. God's Word urges us to pray to God and ask Him to heal us. We back up our prayer with faith that we will have the answer. "The prayer of faith shall save the sick" (Jas. 5:15, KJV).

When we convert our problems into a physical, mental, emotional, or spiritual illness, we not only add to the problems, we also subtract problem-solving strength from ourselves, multiply our difficulties, and divide our capacities. We also endanger our lives.

King Saul had a problem. Samuel was angry at him for disobeying some spiritual orders. The problem was Saul's pride. He needed to repent, change his attitude, and make peace with Samuel. Instead, he developed severe depression and sat in his throne room with headaches, pains, and deep emotional upset. David played his harp and tried to help Saul drive away his depression. Music does have power to alleviate suffering, but King Saul needed more than music. He needed to solve his problem, not convert it into an illness.

Severe mental illness can lead to suicide. Judas Iscariot betrayed Christ. Instead of solving the problem by humbling himself, confessing his sin, and coming back to the

Christ who forgives all, Judas converted his problem into mental illness and killed himself (Matt. 27:5).

The difference between Judas the traitor and Simon Peter the leader was not in the problem of their mutual denial of Christ. Simon Peter denied Christ and swore that he never knew him. This is an example of disassociation that was discussed in chapter 3. Judas converted his problem into a mental illness, while Peter disassociated. Neither one faced up to it.

However, when Peter realized he had a problem, he wept bitterly; he humbled himself; he repented, he returned to the Christ; he received forgiveness; and he solved his problem. Judas didn't.

I know a lady who obtained some very good insurance, just in case she was ever disabled. A few things went wrong and she developed a mild case of depression. She collected from her disability insurance, and from that time on the depression worsened and no one has been able to cure her deep affective disorder. I predict that when the insurance runs out she will by then have persuaded herself that she is really sick. The unconscious mind will cooperate and make the person very ill if the benefits are there.

Those who do not accept some responsibility for their own illness are doomed to dissipate their strength in phony sickness while the problems of life go unsolved. Which seems better: to solve a problem or to avoid it by getting sick?

Negativism

The windowpane of negative transfer has a second technique for converting a problem into another dynamic. It is called negativism. It means that instead of solving the problem, we bad-mouth everything in sight.

I have heard that an army travels on its stomach, but a soldier told me, "I walked across Europe with that army, and I say they traveled on their griping and complaining. It was gripe, gripe, gripe every step of the way." Perhaps, when the going is tough, we need to dissipate our anxiety and frustration by complaining. And perhaps there is some truth to the saying that the wheel that squeaks gets the grease. But it has been my experience that griping and complaining often become substitutes for finding a solution. Many times those people who are inadequate and can do nothing themselves spend endless hours developing the fine art of being a critic.

Most of the time, criticism and complaints are destructive. I am certain that God very seldom answers negative prayers. Whining, nagging, squeaking wheels are more likely to get abandoned than greased. It is legitimate to say, "I need grease; I need help. I have a problem." But when we say, " You are always picking on me," "Nothing ever goes right," "Everyone else is making it but me!" or the classic, "What did I do to deserve this?" the question ends up as negative curses. Cursing is not constructive but destructive.

Negativism does not solve problems; in fact, it causes problems.

People intuitively know that negativism is injurious. That's why we boo the opposition and cheer our team in the game of life. We instinctively know that people do not do well when they are shamed, made to feel guilty, or are harshly criticized for their performance. Occasionally, a sharp prod makes the horse run faster, but beating will only make the horse rear and neigh.

Science has found that children learn faster when we encourage them and hold out a reward than when we hold out a whip. The greyhound runs for the rabbit. The rabbit runs for the carrot. We humans also press ourselves hard for positive rewards. "Come on, you can do it" is the best motivator ever discovered.

Negativism does not solve problems; in fact, it causes problems. Even though, on occasion, the only way we can get the pyramids built is through a whip, the whip alone without rewards will not work.

Cecil B. DeMille directed the movie classic, *The Ten Commandments*, in which Charleton Heston played the role of Moses. While Moses was in favor in Pharaoh's kingdom, he fed the slaves and was able to finish the city of Ramses. He rewarded them, encouraged them, and they built the city. But when the taskmasters beat them and killed them, the slaves destroyed the city. One scene in the movie shows Moses holding up a brick to Pharaoh and saying, "Dead slaves don't make bricks."

The pall of gloom that comes from the negative spirit fills the air and strangles even the strongest.

The most efficient way to kill a person's spirit is to be negative—to harp and carp with negativism. The pall of gloom that comes from the negative spirit fills the air and strangles even the strongest. Problems do not bow to a negative attack. Instead, problems respond to negativism as though it were fertilizer, and they grow like a plot of wild seeds. If you want a lot of problems, then allow yourself to become negative. The icy defense mechanism of negativism doesn't melt one centimeter of the frosty wall of life's problems.

If after almost fifty years of counseling, someone would ask me what is the most prevalent of all human disturbances, I would quickly answer, "negativism." When a person starts counting curses instead of blessings, over-responding to the bad events while ignoring the good events, they give up their joy of living and become sick, not with a physical sickness, but with a combination of mental, emotional, and spiritual sickness. The negative person loses the glow of contentment and takes on the pall of gloom. The principal reason seems to be that they prefer to say, "Ain't it awful," instead of counting their blessings.

The negative person loses the glow of contentment and takes on the pall of gloom. The principal reason seems to be that they prefer to say, "Ain't it awful," instead of counting their blessings.

Matthew 23 records a battle between Jesus Christ, the most positive man who ever lived, and the Pharisees, the world's greatest evil sniffers. No matter what anyone did, it was not good enough for the Pharisees. They loaded impossible burdens on people's backs. Jesus teaches His followers to look for solutions, to count blessings, to be enthusiastic, to have faith, to believe that nothing is impossible with God, and that God loves us and will help us. Those who choose the defense mechanism of negativism can be effective in destroying the most positive program that ever existed.

Reaction Formation

The third way of using the windowpane of negative transfer is called reaction formation, in which threatening problems are denied by emphasizing the opposite extreme.

For example, to conceal prejudice, one may preach tolerance. To deny feelings of rejection, a mother may be over-accepting and indulgent toward her child. The professional defender of public morals may get a great deal of satisfaction from reading the literature or seeing the films he so roundly condemns.

Suppose that in order to clean up pornography in our community, we ask one of the most vigorous complainers to head our committee. If the complainer's aversion to pornography is a reaction formation, he secretly will be attracted to it. He will be a poor choice to lead the committee. On one hand he might try to eliminate pornography, while on the other hand he will strive to indulge his need for it. Such a person will scuttle the best problem-solving committee.

If the man were honest, he might say, "I want pornography out of this community for the sake of my children and my neighbor's children, even for the sake of myself. I am attracted to pornography. I don't want it easily available." Such an honest statement allows us to face the problem. Emotional heat generated by duplicity will camouflage the nature of the problem and hence block the solution.

One day I invited a friend to my group therapy class of convicts. He was dressed in the latest designer fashions. One of the convicts made an improper suggestion to my guest, who was highly incensed that anyone would think him to be a homosexual. The convict responded, "If you're so opposed to homosexuals, why do you dress like one?"

When a problem presents itself, we must remember that in order for the problem to have found us, we are probably sending out some signals of attraction. When we mask our contribution to attracting the problem, we block our ability to solve it.

A young woman went on and on about a certain egotistical, self-centered, cruel football player she was dating. She berated him so vigorously that I suspected a reaction formation, so I confronted her: "I didn't realize you loved the man."

She responded with an outburst of tears, "I hate him, I hate him, I hate him." But we both knew that the unstated problem was that she loved him but felt rejected by him. As long as the reaction formation existed, all she could do was to emote. A reaction formation masks the nature of the problem by declaring that an opposite condition exists. But as soon as our attraction to the object is admitted, we can then honestly search for a solution.

One of the most provocative Scriptures is the statement of Jesus, "Not everyone who says to me, 'Lord, Lord,' will enter the kingdom of heaven" (Matt. 7:21, NIV). God knows the difference between a genuine "Lord, I love you," and a reaction formation whose words say one thing and whose spirit says another.

One day Jesus was very hungry, and in the distance he saw a fig tree that had many leaves. Everyone knows that the figs and the leaves of a fig tree grow together. So Jesus walked a good distance in the hot sun to get some figs off a tree that was advertising it had some. When Jesus got to the tree, there were no figs. So he did what farmers do: destroy the tree that doesn't produce (Matt. 21:19). Jesus put a curse on the tree that was not producing.

People who use reaction formation grow their life trees with lots of leaves but no figs. They advertise loudly that they have something that they do not have. Not only does such a mechanism fail to solve the problem of feeding the hungry, but it also is likely to get a sound rejection from God. Let the inner man who grows fruit and the outer man who advertises the fruit with leaves be the same person.

A fig tree that advertises what it does not have is likely to be destroyed, and a person who advertises what he does not have will also pay the consequences. At best, he won't solve his problems.

Whenever we discover ourselves becoming furiously angry at any person, place, or thing, we need to ask ourselves if our reaction is genuine or if it is a cover-up for our neurotic attraction.

Summary

The three defense mechanisms in the windowpane of negative transfer—conversion, negativism, and reaction formation—serve only to camouflage the real problem. The first step of problem-solving is to squarely look at the problem that faces us. We need to know all about the problem and its causes in order to solve it.

1. In conversion, we get sick.
2. In negativism, we focus on what's wrong.
3. In reaction formation, we conceal attraction by reacting oppositely.

The windowpane of negative transfer not only avoids problem-solving but creates a whole battery of other problems.

Positive Transfer

There comes a time in life when we meet a problem too big for us to solve. No one has yet come up with a solution to cancer, multiple sclerosis, war, poverty, or death. So, when we find ourselves with a life-challenging problem that we can't solve, we can practice "The Windowpane of Positive Transfer" which consists of turning our attention in another direction.

You may ask why I list positive transfer as a windowpane when it may actually solve problems? This book is on how to solve the presenting or main problems of life. When we are presented with a problem, we are to find a solution. Positive transfer does not face the presenting problem. It simply attends to another one. I readily admit that it may be the only thing you can do in certain circumstances, but it is still a windowpane because it does not solve the presenting problem.

There are three types of positive transfer: compensation, identification, and sublimation.

Compensation

The first mechanism is compensation. When we feel defeated because we can't solve a problem, we compensate for our defeat by throwing ourselves into another way of achieving. That's really not a bad idea. But as far as the presenting problem goes, it doesn't work any better than denying that it exists.

Compensation does not solve the problem we are assigned to solve but might solve another one. Hence, it is a defense mechanism and not a true problem-solver.

Let's say that you hire someone to remove a tree stump from your front yard for ninety dollars. Instead of removing the stump, the man cuts the grass, trims the hedges, and repairs the broken fence. Then he comes to you for payment and says, "I couldn't remove your tree stump because my equipment broke, but I did cut your grass and trim the hedges and repair your fence. Pay me." The handyman compensated for what he could not do by doing something else. However, most homeowners would be likely to say, "Our agreement was you remove the stump, you get ninety dollars. I didn't hire you to do yard work and repairs."

So, compensation does not solve the problem we are assigned to solve but might solve another one. Hence, it is a defense mechanism and not a true problem-solver.

Several years ago I was in a wheelchair from an accident. I had a dental appointment, and I was trying to get up three steps into the office. My wife and I ended up in a tangled heap on the bottom step. When we finally made it into the office, I was very upset. The dentist said to me, "I can't do anything about your falling down the steps, but I can do something about your teeth. So, open your mouth." The dentist couldn't do anything about my balance problem, but he could take care of my teeth. He worked on the problem that he *could* solve. That's compensation.

When I was a child, I contracted a disease called poliomyelitis, which left me crippled. I spent a lot of time in the hospital, and when I finally got through the thirteen surgeries, I wore braces on both legs and walked with crutches. In high school I was the only crippled kid in a school of five hundred. I developed some problems. One was the feeling of inferiority. To help conquer those bad feelings, I did what psychologists call overcompensation. I was born to be physical. Since the physical was taken away from me, I overcompensated by throwing myself vigorously into the educational system. When in college, I was never content to take an average load. Once I took maximum units at two universities at the same time. I then enrolled in a correspondence course, and I also preached at a rural church. That's called overcompensation—overdoing it to prove you are not inferior. I find myself constantly being tempted to solve problems by beating my wings on the windowpane of positive transfer and its mechanism of compensation.

Many a person has overcompensated because he or she couldn't solve personal problems. As a child, Thomas Edison was considered to be so dull that he was taken out of school and taught at home by his mother. Unknowingly, she nurtured one of the greatest minds of American history. His lack of academic achievement was compensated by a creative, inventive mind.

My father was a strong man who moved furniture, shoveled coal, farmed, and worked on the railroad. He was a sportsman who loved to hunt. When he became old he was unable to do the active things that he had done as a young man. So, he took up woodworking and made some very artistic furniture. Later on, when his body became even weaker, he took up knitting. One of my most prized possessions is a beautiful afghan my father made to compensate for a weak body.

Compensation is not such a bad way to go, but we must face the fact that our original problem is still not solved.

For example, a researcher may be assigned the problem of finding an effective chemical to combat cancer. He experiments with many things that do not work. Suddenly, he finds a marvelous new chemical combination that cures psoriasis. Everyone rises up and calls him blessed at this serendipitous event. He is awarded a Nobel prize for the cure of psoriasis. The problem is that the researcher is quite likely to *stop* and be content with his discovery, while the problem of cancer goes unsolved.

I'm not against compensation; I'm not even against over-compensation. I use these serendipitous techniques myself. But I'll tell you one thing: I've never fully conquered my feelings of inferiority even though I have done a lot of neat things in compensating for those feelings. Compensation is not a solution to the declared problem.

One day George Washington Carver, a famous black scientist, asked God to reveal to him the secrets of the universe. Dr. Carver declared that the Spirit of God spoke to him and said, "Little man, such a question is too big for you to receive the answer. Ask for something more in keeping with your ability to receive." So, he asked God, "How did you make the peanut?" Dr. Carver said that God revealed the chemical construction of the peanut to him, and that led to the discovery of hundreds of new ways to use the peanut. Dr. Carver virtually revolutionized the agricultural industry of the South by utilizing the technique of compensation.

George Washington Carver did not find out what he wanted to know. The secrets of the universe have not yet been fully revealed to anyone. But, he compensated and found out the secrets of the peanut. Compensation is a good way to go as long as you remember that the solution to the original problem has not yet been found.

Compensation is a good way to go as long as you remember that the solution to the original problem has not yet been found.

Identification

The second positive transfer is identification. We can't solve our problems and so we feel defeated. We identify or associate with someone who does solve problems so that we will feel successful.

Identification can be quite positive, even if it does not solve a presenting problem. For example, a young man might have a great deal of difficulty getting along at home. He may be put down, rejected or even assaulted by his parents. Then he identifies with a youth gang, where his need for acceptance is fulfilled. It is possible for some groups to have a beneficial effect—groups that we find in church or the army or others. Usually, when we join a group or identify with another set of people, we only take our original problems with us.

When gang leaders identify with a positive hero, they sometimes change their behavior. But more often, delinquents identify with anti-hero characters who encourage their admirers to "do their own thing" at the expense of others.

Frequently, marriage is an identification. Marriage is a wonderful institution, but if a girl leaves home to get away from her mother because of dominance problems, the same problems will often surface in her own marriage. Actually, identification is an elaborate method of retreating from the problem, but it can have the positive aspects of getting one out of the present set of problems.

Identification is a natural process in which children at various ages imitate some hero-type. Hopefully, children will imitate their parents. When a father and mother do not provide good images or they make themselves unavailable or are cruel, the child will not be able to identify successfully with them. When the growing child has difficulty assimilating the parents' values, he will often reject them and find a group to identify with.

Whenever a child or an adult gets fixed on certain negative personality types or lifestyles that lessen motivation and encourage narcissism, then identification is damaging. However, for someone to identify with a group like a church or Alcoholics Anonymous is often the first step toward solving some very difficult problems.

I always caution the person that we are put on this earth to solve problems, not to let some group solve them for us.

Though I have listed identification as a windowpane, I do recommend it for a person who needs lots of support and has difficulty making a personal decision. In doing this, I always caution the person that we are put on this earth to solve problems, not to let some group solve them for us. We all need some help from other people, however, and there are times in our life in which we are completely dependent upon others.

In terms of personal problems, identification does not really work—it's a windowpane. Every man, woman, boy, and girl on the face of this earth has been assigned some tasks. In these tasks are some problems. Personal problems require personal attention, and to run away and let a group take over can be dangerous.

In Jesus' day there was a thief and terrorist whose name was Barabbas. He was so popular that the crowds yelled for him to be released from prison instead of Jesus. Evidently they identified with his plan to overthrow the Roman Empire by terrorist activities. If they had chosen Jesus, he would have taught them how to solve their problems through love and self-control. Identifying with an evil leader causes you problems, but choosing Jesus will make you a strong problem-solver.

Identification is a substitute for solving problems. If a young man solves his problem of finding a job by joining the navy, he does solve the problem temporarily, but postpones the true solution for a later date. Since he will be older and more trained, identification possibly was the beginning of a solution for his finding a job.

On the other hand, those who practice identification to its extreme and join a commune seem to believe that all they have to do is be faithful to their little group, roll up in a fetal ball, put their thumbs in their mouths and let "Big Daddy Warbucks" take care of the problem. This extreme type of identification is often harmful rather than helpful. There are some beautiful doors, but identification is not one of them. It's still a windowpane.

Sublimation

The third mechanism under positive transfer is the most useful of the three. Sublimation is using the energy generated by the frustration of the unsolved problem and applying it to another project. Compensation shifts the emphasis from one problem to another, while sublimation uses the power of the original problem to produce answers.

Here is the final defense mechanism, the final way that does not work to solve the problem assigned. However, sublimation is by far the most alluring windowpane of all. It has a few neatly drilled holes in the pane so that the poor bee can find a way through if it persists. Sublimation is not an open door. It is a "substitute open door." Of all the windowpanes, it is the best substitute we have. It is, nevertheless, a substitute.

> *Sublimation is not an open door. It is a "substitute open door." Of all the windowpanes, it is the best substitute we have. It is, nevertheless, a substitute.*

Michelangelo was a brilliant artist who painted his genius on the Sistine Chapel. From some of his writings, there is an implication that he had homosexual tendencies. Perhaps Michelangelo was a latent homosexual. Did he ever solve this problem? Probably not. What did he do about it? Instead of conquering the problem or fulfilling his desires for homosexuality, Michelangelo practiced sublimation. He lay on his back in the scaffolding of the Sistine Chapel and painted magnificent pictures of nude males. The creation story by Michelangelo can certainly be listed as one of the greatest paintings of all time, born out of his marvelous talent, his hard work, his dedication, and his sublimation. His homosexual desire was sublimated into artistic genius.

Many famous people practiced sublimation. The book *Jane Eyre* is a classic example of one girl's hopes and desires that were transmuted into a superb work of fiction.

We all know someone who acts like a "workaholic." The driven business executive who seems unable to stop working may be sublimating feelings of inadequacy in some area and pouring his "all" into business achievement.

Sublimation does not have to be total or permanent. It may even be used to enhance a situation. One famous novelist uses sublimation as a positive force from the moment he first sits down at the typewriter until his book is finished. For this writer, sublimation is a tool, not a way of life. It results in a keener awareness, an enchanted performance. If this performance becomes the only reason for his existence—the point where sublimation occurs at all levels—it then threatens the quality of his life. No matter what heights his diverted drives have helped him achieve, he becomes a victim of external pressure which stifles the development of his full capacities.

When sublimation is the pivotal point of all life, it is a windowpane. If it is used sparingly, it can be an alternative to an open door, but never quite as good as getting to the root of the matter and actually solving the problem.

Years ago, the *Los Angeles Times* carried a front-page story of sublimation at its best. Terry Fox, a 22-year-old Canadian, decided to run from the Atlantic to the Pacific Coast to raise money for cancer research. That was quite an undertaking considering he had only one leg. He lost that leg in the battle against cancer. Terry dipped his artificial leg in the Atlantic surf and began his heroic run. Halfway across Canada, the cancer overtook his lungs, and he was forced to quit. Shortly afterward, he died.

Terry Fox failed to run from the Atlantic to the Pacific, and he didn't raise $1 million for cancer. Instead, the Canadian people rallied and gave $26 million.

Terry was an heroic example of facing problems through sublimation. Sometimes, it is the only option we have open to us. Terry took the strength from his determination to fight his disease and sublimated it into a run to raise money.

Although this was the only legitimate way Terry Fox could go, it still did not solve his problem of cancer. Someone else will have to take the money Terry raised and solve the problem.

Summary

Let's review all the windowpanes and their defense mechanisms presented in this book by using Terry Fox's problem of cancer. Then let's look at some ways he could have gone that would not have been as fruitful.

■   Terry could have **ignored** the problem. He could have *denied* that he even had a problem. He could have pulled the covers up around him and stayed in bed. He would not have run across Canada in jogging shorts exposing his artificial leg. He could have *repressed* the whole subject of cancer and buried it in his subconscious mind. If Terry had done that, he would have suffered from all manner of peculiar reactions stemming from his decision not to deal with his cancer on a conscious level.

■   He could have **protected** himself from the problem. He could have *defended* himself by saying, "It's not my fault I got cancer." Or he could have *rationalized* and made excuses by saying, "I hurt so bad that I can't run." Or he could have *avoided* the whole subject and said, "I can't do anything about it."

■   Terry Fox could have **retreated** into a state of *fantasy* and daydreamed about being the world's greatest athlete. Perhaps he could have *regressed* into child-like behavior, curled up into a fetal ball, become passively dependent and called upon the world to take care of "this poor person with a terrible disease." Or perhaps he could have *dissassociated* and lived as if the cancer did not exist.

■   Terry could have handled his problem by establishing **blame** for the cancer. He could have *introjected* and blamed himself for his condition. He could have *projected*, attacking everyone around him, blaming his mother or his father or the doctors or someone else. Terry could have *displaced* and allowed the fire of anger to burn down into the smoldering coals of resentment and hate, resulting in a futility that lashed out at everything.

■ Terry might have handled his problems through the windowpane of **negative transfer.** He could have *converted* cancer into a mental illness like schizophrenia that retreats from reality. He could have become very *negative* and spent his days complaining about everything. Or Terry could have been consumed by a *reaction formation* and emotionally attacked all cancer researchers. Along with cancer, he could have acquired almost every sickness known to man.

I am happy that Terry Fox did not deny he had a problem or defend himself from facing his problem or daydream or regress. It pleases me that Terry did not attack or blame anyone or convert his problem into another illness. He did not repress it, disassociate himself from it or become negative. How pleasing it is to see a young man face his problems, instead of expending his strength in a reaction formation of emotionality.

■ In the last windowpane of **positive transfer,** Terry could have lost himself in *compensation* by developing strong arms to make up for weak legs. He could have *identified* with some organization or latched onto a hero, but instead, he *became* a hero.

What Terry *did* was to *sublimate* the energy from the terrible condition and put it to good use to raise money to solve the problem. I don't list sublimation as a problem-solving technique because it is one-half windowpane and one-half open door. It is still a defense mechanism because it doesn't solve the original problem, but it does solve a problem that needs to be solved before the major problem can reach a solution. Terry raised money to fight cancer, but he died of his cancer. Sometimes the only way we can solve a problem is to glory in sublimation.

In these six chapters, we have considered six conventional ways people use to attempt to solve problems. They don't work because they do not deal with the primary problem. We can't fly through those windowpanes.

What, then, *can* we do?

The answer is plain—we must face our problems. It is now time to reach for the open doors of *solutions* and fly free into the bright sunlight of answers. The next seven chapters will teach you how to work out your problems, how to harness your emotional energy, and how to glory in your victories for a fruitful, fulfilling lifestyle.

PART 2

Open Doors: Successful Problem-Solving Techniques

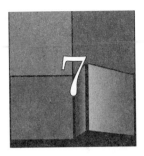

Defining

It is a part of my theory of personality that God places humans on this earth to be tested—to be tried and refined by being presented with problems. Working on the solutions to problems develops character, intelligence, and the graceful awareness of the blessings of God; so, one of the reasons we exist is to try to solve problems.

The first two open doors of defining and opting are for small problems. Simple methods are used for simple problems—use a flyswatter to kill a fly. Some problems fade away with a gentle swat, as in "The Open Door of Defining." We face it, describe it and analyze it—and the solution just naturally presents itself.

Each chapter increases the power of problem-solving techniques. It is important to remember not to use excessive power on a small problem. Doing so throws a person into the hysterical neurosis of over-responding and will quickly make all problems worse. To shoot at a fly with a cannon may kill the fly, but it may also knock the house down.

It is a part of my theory of personality that God places humans on this earth to be tested—to be tried and refined by being presented with problems.

Defining is the first of six doors that we can fly through to help solve some of the problems life hands us. If we're going to solve a problem, there's no substitute for knowing what the problem is. Under the light of careful scrutiny, the elephant of an undefined problem may become a swattable fly. We must take three steps to define a problem:

Step 1: Face It

Back to my story of the bee at the windowpane. The bee seems to be oblivious to the idea that the glass is not a way back to the hive. The bee, like some humans, doesn't seem to realize that a problem exists. So our first step becomes recognition that we have a problem, which consists of three substeps:

1. Admit you have a problem.
2. Accept the problem.
3. Determine to solve it.

When we admit that the way we are doing things is not working, we can then accept the fact that a problem exists. Then we can determine to put our strength into the solution.

For example, the solution to a drinking problem evades all efforts until the alcoholic says clearly and plainly, "I have a problem."

First, the idea is to stop, look, and listen to the problem. I have seen little children when they were teased hold their hands over their ears, close their eyes, and say, "Yah, yah, yah, yah, yah." They didn't want to look at or listen to what the other person was saying. Adults often do the same thing when they want to ignore a problem.

When we admit that the way we are doing things is not working, we can then accept the fact that a problem exists.

Examples are easy to come by. My wife and I know a man who is secretly afraid that he has a terminal disease. He doesn't want to go to the doctor because he doesn't want to hear any bad news. So, he closes his eyes, stops up his ears and says, "Yah, yah, yah, yah, yah," hoping it will go away. If it isn't real, it will go away; but if it *is* real, the sooner he faces it, the better.

Another man I know has run out of money. The rent is coming due in ten days. There will be nothing left for groceries in five. The gas will be turned off tomorrow. But today he lies in bed, numbing his brain with endless bottles of beer and TV shows so that he won't have to face the problem. He seems *not* to know that facing his problems is just a part of life.

In the film, *Shane*, there is a provocative scene in which the farmer straps on his gun to face the ranchers who are trying to drive him off his land. Shane, the retired gunfighter, says to the farmer, "You don't have a chance against their professional gunfighter." The farmer responds, "I have no choice. It's my responsibility. If I can't beat him, then I'll outlast him."

The enemy will not go away. It is time to stand and fight. If we are to solve our problems, we can no longer run or hide or procrastinate. Now is the time to stop whatever we're doing (particularly if it's running away), look over the problem, and listen to its growls. The enemy may not be as fierce as we think. Things that "go bump in the night" are often innocent, natural events. When we stop running, take a good look, and listen closely, the scare usually is no longer a problem.

If we are to solve our problems, we can no longer run or hide or procrastinate.

Why is it that people procrastinate solving their problems and try to fly through closed windows? I suppose it is because they're afraid—afraid that the problem may live up to their worst expectations. I am reminded of the classic statement Franklin Roosevelt made when the nation was in the throes of a frightening depression: "The only thing we have to fear is fear itself." That's the truth. Problems are a part of our natural heritage. We are built to be magnificent problem-solving creatures. We never need to be afraid of a problem, but we need to be deathly afraid of not facing the problem.

When I began to teach the Dale Carnegie Course many years ago, Mr. Carnegie encouraged people who were afraid to speak up in public by saying, "Do the thing you fear, and the death of fear is certain." That principle enabled a lot of people to get on their feet in front of a class.

Once we decide to admit we have a problem and to accept it as our task, then we must determine to solve the problem. Acceptance is a noble practice, particularly acceptance of those things we can't change. But solving problems is a major purpose of life, and no one can or will feel fulfilled if they do not make an attempt to solve the problems that life, circumstance, and God present to them.

We never need to be afraid of a problem, but we need to be deathly afraid of not facing the problem.

General Toulare was shaving at 5:00 in the morning just before the Battle of Tours. He cut himself and was heard by an aide to remark, "Tremblest thou, vile carcass? Thou wouldst tremble even more if thou knewest where I am taking thee today." The general did not let his fears control him. Even if his body trembled, he was not going to do what the body wanted him to do. He was going to do what his will and determination had conceived as the right way.

It doesn't make any difference if our body is trembling with fear. If we have been assigned a problem, we must face it, look it over, and determine what the size of our opposition might be. Under a broad, steady look in the light of day, as seen through the eyes of the bold, most problems assume small dimensions.

Step 2: Describe It

The second step in the open door of defining is to describe the problem. We have stopped running and have stopped defending ourselves. We are no longer beating ourselves against a closed window. We have bravely turned around and are looking our problem over.

When the children of Israel were poised at the Jordan River, waiting to go into the land that God had promised them, they sent twelve spies to assess the problems of invasion. When the spies came back to Moses, ten of them described the land that had been promised them in such terms that they made the people feel it was impossible to occupy the land. Two of the spies described the land as a wonderful place and stated, "We are well able to take it." Unfortunately, the people accepted the gloomy description of the land. They saw themselves as being merely grasshoppers in a land occupied by giants. So they wandered in the wilderness for forty years until a new generation could arise that could describe their problems in a positive, directive way that could lead toward a solution.

The three phases in describing our problem consist of:

1. Naming your problem.
2. Stating it in a noncircular way.
3. Making it hopeful.

To solve our problems, we must recognize what they are and call them by name.

The first phase of describing your problem can easily be accomplished by asking yourself the question, "What is the problem?" It is amazing how many times I hear people say, "I don't know what's wrong." To solve our problems, we must recognize what they are and call them by name.

In the beginning, God asked Adam to name the animals. He also asked Adam to take dominion over the animals. In other words, in order to solve the problem of taking dominion, we must first name what we intend to dominate. That's what we do with our problems. After we've accepted them, we name them.

In the second phase of describing the problem, we state it in a noncircular way. In answering the question, "What is the problem?" the tendency is to answer the question with another question. This becomes a subtle way of avoiding the problem.

For example, if I ask the question, "What is the problem?" and then answer it by saying, "Why don't I have enough money?" I have answered a question with a question—it becomes circular. It doesn't lead to a solution, but it goes back to the original question. Hence, it is difficult to solve the problem. So, when I try to name the problem by asking the question, "What is the problem?" I must answer it with an affirmative statement that will lead toward a solution.

Instead of answering the question, "What is the problem?" by saying, "Why don't we have enough money?" we state it declaratively: "We don't have enough money." There are many declarative statements that describe the problem in a way that leads to a solution instead of a circle back to the question.

- "We are charging too many things on credit cards."

- "We are not talking over our credit card purchases."

- "We are spending money on unnecessary items."

- "We don't have a plan for spending our money."

- "We are not sticking to our budget."

- "We are not earning enough money."

Jay Haley, in his book *Problem-Solving Therapy* (2nd ed. [Jossey-Bass San Francisco, 1987]), addresses the problem of circular thinking in a similar way. He says that we need to put a problem in a form that makes it solvable. Concerning problems in counseling:

> If a family should say, "Why is mom too anxious?" that is not a solvable problem. The ways in which this anxiety manifests itself and the response to it are the problem. Seldom are traditional diagnostic categories a solvable problem. To say the problem is "schizophrenia" or "mental retardation" is to say nothing related to therapy. "Identity confusion" or "low self-esteem" or "depression" or most of the terminology of psycho-

dynamic language is not useful when one is formulating a problem. A "school phobia" is not a problem one can resolve, but a child who will not go to school is an operational problem. Problems, whether one calls them symptoms or complaints, should be something one can count, observe, measure or in some way know one is influencing.

I agree with Dr. Haley. We need to be certain when we state a problem that it does not come back on itself in an unanswerable way. The statement of the problem must contain some elements of solution or there is no use to state the problem. To say, "Why don't I have enough money?" is unanswerable. To say, "Presently, I don't have enough money," has within it a solution because we now can count how much is enough, and ask other questions. When the statement of the problem itself is the question, it does not lead to an answer.

When stating the problem, be sure there is something you can count or observe or measure or in some way do something about.

When stating the problem, be sure there is something you can count or observe or measure or in some way do something about.

Phase three of describing the problem is to make it hopeful. There is a major trap in describing a problem in such a negative way that it takes the hope out of the answer. Even though we have named the problem in a declarative way, we must make certain that the declaration is not just a hopeless one, but that it includes positive factors that lead toward a solution.

For example, suppose we answer our original question, "What is the problem?" in a declarative way that is negative. We might say, "I just can't seem to get going," or, "I don't know what's wrong; everything's against me," or, "I don't know how to succeed," or, "No one helps me," or, "I always have bad luck." All these statements and a thousand more like them have no answer because they are hopeless. They don't lead to a solution because they suggest that the problem is too big for a solution.

When we answer the question, "What is the problem?" it should lead to a solution, not to a question that dead ends or to a negative complaint that is a disguised form of griping. That process becomes a defense mechanism against actually doing something constructive. We need to describe our problem in a noncircular, positive, hopeful way that leads to a solution.

Here are some examples of describing a problem by making it noncircular and hopeful instead of circular and negative.

Circular: "Why don't I have enough money?"
Noncircular: "Presently, I don't have enough money."
Negative: "I can never make enough money."
Hopeful: "My present job doesn't pay me enough money."

Can you do something about the hopeful, directive statement? Yes, you can.

Another problem:

Circular: "Why does Johnny get such low grades?"
Noncircular: "Right now Johnny gets poor grades in school."
Negative: "Johnny always was a poor student."
Hopeful: "Since Johnny got a car, his grades have been poor."

The hopeful, noncircular way is a truthful, declarative sentence that leads easily to possible solutions.

Another example:

Circular: "Why doesn't my wife talk to me?"
Noncircular: "Recently, my wife doesn't communicate."

Negative: "My wife will never communicate."

Hopeful: "My wife doesn't talk to me when I'm late for dinner."

The hopeful, directive way immediately tells me what I can do to solve the problem. What is the problem? When we state the problem in a noncircular, hopeful, directive way, we have a forward step toward solution, not a backward step.

I may state a problem, "My marriage needs new vitality." If that is true, then it leads to many things I could do about it. If I state the same problem in an unanswerable way, "Why does my wife hate me?" then the very question and the way it was stated so negatively prevent an ongoing solution. The only way problems can be solved is to (1) face them and (2) describe them in a way that gives hope, not despair.

There is no answer when we say, "Why do I have terminal cancer?" We have the hope of survival when we say, "My doctors and I are fighting the problem of cancer." "Why do I have this impossible insomnia?" can be stated, "I need to find better ways of getting to sleep." "Why has my marriage ended in divorce?" has given up the fight, while "I need to find ways to save my marriage" provides the beginning of answers.

The Spanish language has a great way of expressing this concept. The verb "to be" has two words: *ser* and *estar.*

Ser is the permanent form of "to be" and is applied to unchanging things, like I am (ser) a male. But when I talk about changeable things like how I feel, I use *estar*: I am (estar) sad. (I may not be sad tomorrow.) Estar has within it the hope of change. Ser is fixed. For a problem to be solved, it must have within it the hope of change. We Christians call that *faith* and *hope.*

Several prophets of God had trouble with circular questions and negative thinking. It took an act of heaven itself to get them to solve their problems and change the circular and the negative into the directive and the positive.

The great prophet Isaiah, for example, had a problem. He said, "In the year that King Uzziah died, I saw the Lord seated on a throne, high and exalted, and the train of his robe filled the temple" (Isa. 6:1, NIV). God was asking him to preach His message. But Isaiah cried, "Woe is me! for I am undone; because I am a man of unclean lips, and I dwell in the midst of a people of unclean lips" (Isa. 6:5, KJV). What a negative response to the high calling of God! So God sent an angel with a live coal from the altar to touch Isaiah's mouth saying, "Your iniquity is taken away and your sin is purged" (Isa. 6:7, NASB). Then Isaiah could say to the call of God, "Here am I. Send me" (v. 8, NASB).

Several prophets of God had trouble with circular questions and negative thinking. It took an act of heaven itself to get them to solve their problems and change the circular and the negative into the directive and the positive.

We too can turn our negative complaints (Woe is me), and our circular reasoning (why am I a man of unclean lips?) into a positive answer (Here am I) and a straightforward declaration (Send me). When we see that God wants us to solve our problems, perhaps we can begin by defining the problem in a straightforward, positive way.

Moses, another prophet of God, was asked to go to Pharaoh to get the Israelites released. Moses defined the problem in a negative, circular way. He said, "Who am I, that I should go to Pharaoh?" (Ex. 3:11, NIV). Even when God told him that he would be with him, Moses continued to make excuses. "I'm not a good speaker, and Pharaoh won't listen to me" (paraphrased). The problem was solved only by God

Himself addressing it in a declarative, positive way. He instilled confidence in Moses by giving him special powers and an assistant to confront Pharaoh.

We may not receive a special emissary from heaven to help us solve our problems. If we did receive one, what he would do is change our negative thinking and circular reasoning like he did for Isaiah and Moses so that we could positively address and declaratively express our problems. We don't need an angel. We can do that now with the help of the Holy Spirit. So instead of asking God for some special action, let's trust God to help us express our problems in a way that we also may come to solution.

Step 3: Analyze It

The third step of the open door of defining is to analyze the problem. Analyzing the problem consists of three phases:

1. Ask yourself the causes of the problem.
2. Rank the causes in order of importance.
3. Search for the causes of each cause.

Let's take the phases one step at a time. There are many causes to any problem. Suppose my stated problem is "I have a cold." The causes could be:

- "I was around people with colds."
- "I was not eating properly."
- "I didn't take my vitamins."
- "I was emotionally upset."
- "I was not getting proper rest."

The simple problem of "I have a cold" may have many causes.

If we say, "Our business is not taking in enough money per month," we would be describing a problem. In the first phase of analyzing the problem, we would answer the question "What causes the problem?" with such causes as:

- "We have too many charge accounts."
- "Our overhead is too high."
- "We don't make enough sales."
- "We don't have enough salespeople."

The second phase under the step of analyzing is to rank the causes in order of importance. In the causes above, we may rank "don't have enough salespeople" as first and "don't make enough sales" as second, "overhead is too high" as third, and "too many charge accounts" as fourth. So we arrange our causes in order of importance.

Now, we take the third step in analyzing the problem and ask ourselves the question "What are the causes of each cause in order of importance?" Since I have ranked "don't have enough salespeople" as first, I will then make a list of the reasons for this cause. The reasons may be such things as:

- "We have not advertised to hire more salespeople."
- "Our commission structure does not give enough percentage to the salespeople."
- "Our product is not glamorous enough to attract salespeople."
- "We have no sales manager to train salespeople."

One of the reasons or causes of the cause will lend itself to immediate solution. We may look at the above four causes of the cause and decide that we need a sales manager. So, we hire one. He proceeds to hire salespeople, and our business begins to prosper. We have found at least one answer to the original question, "What is the problem?" and its declarative statement, "Our business is not taking in enough money per month."

Let's take a problem from the beginning through the three steps of analyzing. Let's suppose that one of our children is having trouble at school. I have discussed Tim's problems with the teacher long enough. I now decide that we do have a problem. I admit it. I accept it. And I am determined to solve it.

Second, I describe it by asking myself the question "What is the problem?" I do this in a declarative way to avoid circular reasoning: "My son is now having trouble at school." And I state this declaration in a hopeful way that leads to a solution: "The principal thinks we can solve Tim's problems at school."

Third, I analyze the problem by asking myself the question, "What are the causes of this problem?" I make a list of the causes. Then I rank them in order of importance. They may be:

- "My son never brings home homework."
- "My son is preoccupied with his girlfriend."
- "My son spends too much time driving his car."
- "My son is too involved in sports."
- "My son is lazy."

There can be many causes of the problem. But for the sake of analyzing and reaching a solution, we take one of the causes which we believe to be of first importance: "My son never brings home homework." Now we can break this cause down into subcauses. We now ask ourselves the question, "What causes the cause?" or, "Why does he do that?" We may answer:

- "We do not encourage Tim to do his homework."
- "Tim doesn't want to do homework."
- "Tim is more interested in his car."
- "Tim is more interested in his girlfriend."
- "Tim is indifferent to homework."

We may find a dozen causes of the cause. One of the causes will lend itself to a solution. Suppose we choose the subcause of "We do not encourage Tim to do his homework." The answer may simply be to talk to him and encourage him. If we do not find the solution, we can go back to the problem and look at the second cause on our list of priorities which is, "My son is too preoccupied with his girlfriend." Again, what are the causes of this cause?

We keep going down our list of the causes of the problem and break each cause down into a list of causes. When you name the causes of the cause you are very close to the naming of a solution.

Summary

Let's review the steps in the open door of defining the problem.

- Step 1: Face the problem. It belongs to you. Don't run and hide.

- Step 2: Describe the problem. You need to know as much about it as you possibly can. Ask yourself the question, "What is the problem?" State the answer to that question in a hopeful, noncircular way. Don't answer a question with a question, and don't make your answer a negative complaint.

- Step 3: Analyze the problem by asking yourself the question, "What are the causes of the problem?" Then arrange the causes in a logical priority. Take the chief cause and ask the question, "What causes the cause?"

You have now looked at the problem from many angles. This easy way of defining the problem should bring most of the solutions quickly to mind.

The majority of the time, we need to go no further than through the open door of defining. Once we know what the problem is, what its causes are, what its chief cause might be and what caused that cause, we have taken an analysis back to the third dimension, and the solution, most of the time, will be as easy as a bee flying through an open door.

If after applying the formulas presented in the first two open doors of defining and opting, the problem still persists, then, we can bring out the bigger guns.

Opting

When we face a mountain, there are thousands of ways to climb it. There is, of course, the best way, but no one has 20-20 foresight. To scale the mountain-sized problem, we need to consider "The Open Door of Opting" and its three steps: consider and list every alternative, choose the best possible solution, and take action.

Consider and List Every Alternative

Remember the bee beating its wings futilely against the windowpane? The bee had a beautiful alternative: turn around and fly in the other direction. There was a way out of the dilemma, but the way the bee was going was not the way out. To the bee, the windowpane looked like clear air. It just didn't have enough sense to figure things out. So it stubbornly pressed forward, unable to consider the alternatives. Humans are really lucky. God gave us a magnificent brain that *can* consider alternatives.

The lemming and the army ant are two unique creatures that illustrate the concept of opting. When a population explosion comes to the lemming, thousands of these little furry, squirrel-like creatures throw themselves off a cliff into the ocean and swim to their certain suicide. In contrast, the army ants march across the land to establish another colony. When they come to a river, they too could throw themselves into the stream and promptly die by the millions. But these smart little creatures have discovered an alternative. What do they do? They climb a tree and with their sharp pincers cut off a leaf. Then a dozen or so climb on the leaf and ride across the stream to establish a home on the other side.

When we face a mountain, there are thousands of ways to climb it. There is, of course, the best way, but no one has 20-20 foresight.

In World War II when the Germans decided to invade France, they didn't throw endless German men against the Maginot Line to die like lemmings before the concrete and steel fortresses. They simply took a small Panzer corps and went around the line. Their ability to opt for another alternative temporarily cost France her freedom.

Some of my clients get really angry with me if I suggest that there's another way out besides that dead-end windowpane. Some of us, like the lemmings, throw ourselves into the sea of absolutisms; and no matter how hard we swim we eventually die because there is no end to that sea. It doesn't make any difference what the excuse might be; solutions that lead to death, failure, misery and unhappiness are not solutions. The test of our ability to survive is the test of our ability to use alternative ways to get to the top.

Often in counseling, people have painted themselves into a corner. Geneva was such a client. She had severe headaches that were caused by her overinvolvement with her daughter, Teresa. Teresa loved horses and didn't care to socialize with people much. Geneva was so worried about Teresa not having friends that she would get tension headaches.

Geneva had only one way of approaching the problem, which was to try to force Teresa to socialize. If Teresa didn't, Geneva would get sick, and that made Teresa withdraw from people even more. Geneva was in a no-win situation. She felt that to be a good mother, she must invest all of her energies into Teresa's perceived problem. When she did that, she got a headache. If she didn't respond to Teresa, she felt she was a bad mother.

If you can't make a list of alternatives or solutions to the causes of your problem, then put it down in your little red book as a positive fact: you are beating your wings against a windowpane

I taught her to opt for other alternatives. She discovered that a "good" mother could have a loving response without tension. She learned to handle her emotions with minimal stress and strain through prayer, relaxation, meditation, and learning the biblical principles of trust and thinking on uplifting things.

If we want to win in the game of life, we must be able to consider alternative solutions, and this step of listing solutions to the problem is the most important step of all. If you can't make a list of alternatives or solutions to the causes of your problem, then put it down in your little red book as a positive fact: you are beating your wings against a windowpane, and the absolute way you think you must go will send you with the lemmings, drowned in the open sea.

How do we get a list of alternatives or solutions to a problem?

Brainstorm. Brainstorming is effective because it allows our imagination to come up with unusual and unique solutions. In this step to problem-solving, we need to consider every solution that comes to our minds even if it seems farfetched. Creative thinking is the mark of an intelligent person. Write down every possible or impossible solution that crosses your mind, even the wild ideas. Some people are so practical minded that they ignore a possible way-out solution or alternative to solving the problem.

For example, when General MacArthur was planning to invade a city in Korea, one of his aides said, "It is impossible to go this way," pointing to a sea wall. General MacArthur replied, "That's what the enemy thinks, so that's the way we'll go." That's what brainstorming is: considering the possibility of the impossible.

Dream a little. Imagine you have more money, more power, more wisdom than you really have. Say to yourself, "If I had____then I would____." Constructive dreaming often follows a fantasy. Without fantasy, constructive dreaming would bog down. A famous man once said, "Imagination begins in fantasy and ends in creativity." Do not be afraid to dream great dreams and to think great thoughts. Just don't stop there. Of course, if all we have is fantasy, we then have a defense mechanism. But if we don't have a little fantasy, we can't proceed to creativity.

Ask the experts for possible alternatives. Make a list of the things they suggest. When we are trying to solve a problem, we need to rely heavily on the experience of others who have gone that way before. There is a saying, "Those who ignore history are doomed to repeat it."

Often, we are hesitant to ask experts their opinions. We are afraid that they are too busy or too important. We must remember that one of the major reasons for being alive is helping people. Don't take the experts' reason for existence away from them. You will probably be amazed at how flattered they are to be asked.

One day a client presented me with the problem of compulsive behavior. I studied the subject but still needed more information. I recalled that a professor at a local university had done some cutting-edge work with compulsive behavior. I called the university and persisted until I got his office. His assistant informed me that his boss was a very important, very busy man and that he was sure the the professor would be too busy to return my call. But I persisted. One day I called at the precise moment he was in the office, and to my amazement, the professor was most gracious and helpful. He actually thanked me for calling him. He said, "I miss not having much contact with the world that uses my ideas. I want you to know that you have strengthened and encouraged me by this call. Please call again."

My point is that everyone around an expert tries to protect him or her. The expert is often eager to share with you what he or she has learned. Just be sure you have studied enough to know the right questions to ask.

Ask little children or uninformed people what they would do. The child or the naive often has a solution that the experts cannot see. There is a certain blindness that belongs to the sophisticated and learned that makes them ignore the obvious.

Remember the folk story of "The Emperor's New Clothes"? The emperor was a vain king who wore the finest of clothes made by the best of tailors. One day two rogues persuaded the emperor that they could weave a magic cloth which could be seen only by the wisest and would be invisible to the dull or those unfit for their jobs. No one wished to be called a fool or unfit, so everyone, including the emperor, claimed to see the invisible cloth. One day as he paraded proudly down the avenue displaying his invisible clothes, a child revealed the secret, "But he has nothing on."

"The Emperor's New Clothes" teaches us that the experts can be fooled, while a little child often see the obvious. In attempting to solve problems in your own life, be willing to share your alternatives with the innocent, the naive, the uneducated. Often, they can see what the experts miss.

Reconsider the problem from every angle. Imagine that you are a different person and try to think of the problem from that person's point of view. The man who solved the problem of getting the salmon to use fish ladders at Bonneville Dam said, "The fish wouldn't use the ladders. I began to think from the fish's point of view, and then I knew the ladders needed covers." Think of your problem from other perspectives, even a fish's.

Remember that such a common event as an automobile accident can be viewed from four different corners. And if a helicopter was flying overhead, another view would be possible. Position your mind in every corner that you can imagine to view the event in order to consider alternatives. The bee only looks straight ahead. The Creator placed within us the imagination to occupy another space and look at the problem from another position. Expanding our ways of looking at the problem will certainly expand the alternatives.

Research at your local library. Ask your librarian where you can find the answer to your problem. The Bible tells us, "There is nothing new under the sun" (Eccles. 1:9, NASB). You can be sure that if you have a problem, someone else has wrestled with that same problem and has written down their solutions. Read, study, and research—you will most likely find answers.

I have a friend, Liz, who took a whole day to spend at the library. She said to the reference librarian, "I know you are very busy, but I would like to spend the day learning how the reference library works. Would you be able to get me started?" Liz said she had never been treated so royally. The librarian's eyes lit up and she eagerly showed Liz this file and that abstract section. Once she became familiar with the library, Liz felt comfortable calling once in a while to ask the librarian a specific question that needed an answer. Liz says, "Usually the librarian has been able to help me on the spot." If the librarian is busy, Liz just leaves her phone number and the librarian gets back to her.

I recommend taking a day to visit the library and meet the librarian. I have also found that when I call a library and ask them a question or for a quotation, they are most friendly and will help me find the answer.

Another way to do research is through a personal computer. Those people who have modems on their computers can tap into a number of powerful computer banks. Research is a time-honored method of finding truth, expanding knowledge, and solving problems. The particular methods of research are beyond the scope of this problem-solving book, but the sources are not difficult to find.

Communicate with God. Isaiah 9:6 (NASB) predicts that the coming Messiah will be called "Wonderful Counselor." Jesus and the Holy Spirit can be our Counselor and advise us concerning the solutions to problems. "Everyone who asks, receives" (Luke 11:10, NASB). Ask God for solutions, and then work hard trying to find them. Ask as if prayer would bring the only answer; then work as if your search would bring the only answer. Between your search and the Holy Spirit, how can you lose?

I have some devout friends who only believe in using prayer to God for answers. They use their own intuition and claim that it is the Holy Spirit speaking to them. They also use the idea of "closed doors" and various circumstances and events to make their decisions. In my opinion, they often come up with lopsided views. God uses more than direct communication to guide His children. In addition to the Bible, we have the church, history, tradition, our friends, our family, common sense, nature, good books, our own intelligence, and science. Of course, prayer and the Bible are our first consideration.

I believe that God has assigned us to become problem-solvers. He wants to be consulted. He doesn't want us to become independent from Him, but neither does He want us to be passive children.

Here's how I utilize the internal reference library of the Holy Spirit. I ask God to help me, and then I wait patiently for ideas to form in my head. I sometimes role play. I ask a question as myself and answer the question as if the one who responded were God. Sometimes I do this in written form. I write a letter to God and ask how to solve the problem. I then reverently write an answer from what I think is God's standpoint. I have found some unique and insightful alternatives by using this method.

The above seven methods—to brainstorm, dream a little, ask the experts, ask a little child, consider a different angle, research, and communicate with God—will produce an immense number of alternatives. These possible solutions will prepare us for our next step of problem-solving.

Choose the Best Possible Solution

You are now ready for the second step to the open door of opting, which is to choose the best possible solution.

Go over your list. Hopefully, you have compiled a long list of alternatives, among which are a few impossible ideas. It is your job now to choose one of the possible solutions.

Eliminate impossible solutions. Most of the way-out solutions can be eliminated quickly. Their purpose was to stimulate your thinking. Keep considering and crossing off until you have three to five possible ways to solve the problem.

Ask for help. First from God, then from your friends. You have done your homework. You have the solution to the problem down to three to five alternatives. Ask yourself, "What should I do?" even as you ask God to help you make a decision.

As you ask yourself and God what the best solution might be, you also ask your friends. The people who know you and love you are often very intuitive and can sometimes point the way. I believe that one reason God gave us the church was to have the fellowship of caring people who help each other in time of need.

The members of my Sunday School class really get involved in helping one another solve problems. We deal with such things as "My job is no longer satisfying or lucrative," "I need to change locations," "My mate is sick and I don't know what to do," or, "My friend wants to borrow money." In our Sunday School class, we ask God to help us help each other solve problems, and we are coming up with some pretty good solutions.

Prioritize the possible solutions. Narrow the solution to the problem down to three to five alternatives. To the best of your ability, put the solutions in order of importance.

Now we come to the moment of truth. We must make a decision and *choose the best possible solution* considering the present moment. We know what the problem is. We know what caused it. We have considered some causes of the cause. We have listed alternative solutions. Now, among all those alternatives, we must choose one. The only other factor to consider is that of the here and now. A good solution yesterday and tomorrow may not be a good decision today. So we must look at present factors and prepare to pay the cost. The Bible puts it succinctly, "Estimate the cost" (Luke 14:28, NIV).

Today is the day, and sometimes we can't wait for more favorable circumstances. Considering the day in which we live, we are now ready to do the one thing that is more difficult than any other step—take your chances, pay the price, and choose the best possible solution.

Shakespeare's Hamlet had a terrible time making decisions. He was a perfect character of valor, kindness, strength, and virtue, but he had one tragic flaw—indecisiveness. "To be or not to be . . . " just doesn't get anything done.

A friend said to me, "Well, if I knew which path to take, I'd take it." True, seldom do we know for sure which path to take. Choosing the best that we know is considerably better than being frozen in indecision. If the first solution doesn't work, you can move on to the next alternative.

More businesses have failed and more people have not succeeded for this simple reason: they were afraid to make a decision. So, choose the best possible solution under the present circumstances, and then you are ready to go to the next step.

Choosing the best that we know is considerably better than being frozen in indecision.

Take Action

When you have chosen the best possible solution, put that solution to work immediately. The lack of decisive action is the greatest failure of all.

During the Civil War, Abraham Lincoln wrote a letter to General Meade in which he said, "I do not believe you appreciate the magnitude of the misfortune involved in Lee's escape. He was within our easy grasp, and to have closed upon him would, in connection with our other late successes, have ended the war. As it is, the war will be prolonged indefinitely. If you could not safely attack Lee last Monday, how can you possibly do so south of the river, when you can take with you very few—no more than two-thirds of the forces you then had in hand? Your golden opportunity is gone, and I am distressed immeasurably because of it."

Meade's lack of action cost the lives of thousands of valiant men, and it grieved the president. Our indecisiveness, our failure to take action, often costs us the solutions to life's problems and minimizes our joy and contentment.

I have on my desk a manual entitled *Mental Disorders*. It is a diagnostic and statistical manual of the American Psychiatric Association. One of the major categories of mental illness is called "neurosis," and one of its first symptoms is indecisiveness and a loss of joy of living.

Many times I have clients who cannot be classified as mentally ill, nor are they receiving counseling to improve their quality of life. They are clients who are frozen in a gigantic block of ice, unable to make a decision. I counsel with a young man who has bulimia, the infamous gorge-purge disease. For five years we have known and diagnosed his problem. We have gone over hundreds of possible solutions, and we have chosen, with the help of many experts, the best possible solution to his problem. All George has to do is inaugurate, choose, enact, start, or activate the best possible solution. But he never does. Because of my experience with him and many like him, I consider the step of *activation* to be the crucial one, so I have devoted chapter 13 to taking action.

The inability to make decisions becomes one of the first indicators of growing mental incapacity. Decision-making causes some people such trauma that they pass up outstanding opportunities. Such was the case of Ed who had shoveled coal for twenty years into a furnace at a factory. Because he was getting old, and because the boss felt sorry for him, management decided to give Ed an easier job and pay him more money. They put him on the assembly line separating the bad potatoes from the good potatoes. After three hours of picking out the bad potatoes, the old man begged for his former job of shoveling coal. The boss asked, "Why? Isn't the new job lighter work?"

"Yes."

"Isn't it more pay?"

"Yes."

"Isn't it easier on your back?"

"Yes."

"Then why do you want your old job back?"

"Well, I just can't stand making all those decisions."

This story is really true to life—if you can't stand making decisions, you are likely to remain shoveling coal in this life and perhaps the next one, too. One of the saddest conditions that can come upon a person is the inability to take action. It makes no difference how effectively the other steps are carried out, if the *action* step is not taken, we have wasted our time.

One of the saddest conditions that can come upon a person is the inability to take action. It makes no difference how effectively the other steps are carried out, if the action step is not taken, we have wasted our time.

I heard the story of a famous French general. He was told, "Our right flank is crumbling; our left flank is in retreat; the center is wavering—oh General, what shall we do?" The General responded, "The situation is ripe—attack." Sometimes in the midst of the greatest defeat, an all out positive attack is called for.

Lukewarm, indecisive, middle-of-the-road type people find themselves unable to make an attack to solve problems. When they make a decision, they never know if they will succeed and end up at the top of the heap; but when they don't make a decision, they have guaranteed they will lose and end up at the bottom of the heap.

There are rare times when making no decision *is* the decision. A declared policy to do nothing is sometimes the best way to go, but to do nothing because of default or lack of decisiveness is certain disaster.

Summary

1. Write down every option, solution, or alternative you can find.
2. Choose the best possible solution available under the present circumstances.
3. Take action on your best possible solution, even though it might not be the ultimate answer.

The open doors of defining and opting are the passageways we use when everyday problems confront us. When we define a problem, we face it, describe it and analyze it. In the open door of opting we consider alternate solutions, select the best possible solution, and put it into action.

We use this simple method for simple problems. These flyswatter techniques are all we need to kill a fly. The methods detailed in the next chapters are used when the fly becomes an elephant.

Organizing

Most of the minor problems of life are easily solved by applying the open doors of defining and opting. Occasionally, however, problems don't lend themselves to easy solutions. Problems can become very complex and tied to many extraneous subjects. Problems often involve genetics, environment, circumstances, interpersonal relationships, sociology, psychology, politics, and many other factors. Some problems like war, poverty, and disease have been with the human race since the beginning of time and show very little sign of permanent solution. The last four chapters on open doors are designed to attack long-range, complex problems.

You can use "The Open Door of Organizing" when you come up against a really difficult problem. It has three steps: form a team, make a plan, and practice your strategy.

Form a Team

No one person can possibly build an atomic bomb or launch a missile or run an automobile factory. Some things are just too big for one person. We need the cooperation of others. Rudyard Kipling said, "T'aint the individual or the nation as a whole, but the everlasting teamwork of every blooming soul." We need to form a team.

There is truth to the old joke: "If you throw three Americans out of an airplane three miles above the earth, they will have themselves organized into a committee of president, vice-president and secretary before they hit the ground." Committees may be overused and sometimes are a bore, but they are an efficient tool to solve difficult problems.

Most people enjoy power in their lives. Many want to be the quarterback, the star. But there are no stars without satellites, and there are no quarterbacks without offensive linemen and wide receivers.

Rudyard Kipling said, "T'aint the individual or the nation as a whole, but the everlasting teamwork of every blooming soul." We need to form a team.

We are assigned by the nature of our own responsibility to bear our own burdens. "For every man shall bear his own burden" (Gal. 6:5, KJV). A man must learn to stand on his own two feet and solve his problems. But sometimes it is difficult to do that unless we form a team and learn how to "Bear ye one another's burdens, and so fulfil the law of Christ" (Gal. 6:2, KJV).

Our great corporations have made America the most productive country in the world. These big businesses are

fine examples of teamwork—people working together.
From the team come many stars; but without the team,
there can be no stars. General Motors knows the way to
find the best solution to their problems: they hire a team of
experts. Then they discuss their ideas and develop a plan.
We as individuals can do the same. We even have an
advantage over big business: we don't have to hire a team;
all we have to do is to develop the courage to ask for advice.

You can't form a team without asking for help, so put
your fears in your pocket and realize you're paying that
person a compliment when you trust his or her judgment
enough to ask for help.

Here are some suggestions for organizing:

- Have a well-defined goal, something that is worthwhile to you and others.
- Ask compatible, congenial, knowledgeable friends
  and relatives to serve on a temporary team. If you
  start with people you know and care for and tell them
  it's just for a short while, you should have no trouble
  getting a team of advisors together.
- Using your team of compatible friends and relatives,
  ask them to suggest the names of other people who
  might volunteer their time once in a while to help in
  a worthy cause.
- In forming your team, ask the busiest, most competent people you know. Start at the top, not at the bottom. Busy people are usually intelligent and stable.
  You need both to solve your problem.
- When your team gets together to help you, have an
  agenda. Be friendly, concise, and noncombative. You
  are not there to put anyone down; you are there to
  have people help you solve a problem. Of course, you
  are the chairman of the group. Follow the rule of the
  "3 Bs": be brief, be brilliant, and be seated.
- Remember that the buck stops with you. It is necessary to get people to help you and advise you, but it is

your problem, and you must reserve the decisive vote for yourself.

■ Be enthusiastic, organized, determined, and friendly. To have a team to help you solve that problem, you need to treat them with respect. Listen to them and thank them.

Many people try to solve difficult problems by going from person to person asking opinions. Such a technique does not work. You cannot have a quarterback that plays in New York and a wide receiver that plays in Los Angeles and expect the passes to be completed. The team must play on the same field. The people who advise must get together in one group to receive feedback, to get some consensus of opinion, and to make the synergic principle work.

It is of crucial importance to ask God to be a part of your problem-solving team. ... When we leave God out, we are certain to make mistakes.

Synergism is the power generated when more than one motor or power is attached to the same shaft. The energy generated by eight ten-horse engines on a single crankshaft is much more than just the multiple of 8 x 10. The power of the group working together is the genius of our technology. It will also be the genius of our problem-solving.

Only one more factor needs to be added in forming a team. It is of crucial importance to ask God to be a part of your problem-solving team. When Joshua, captain of the Israeli host, crossed the Jordan River and defeated the cities of Ai and Jericho, the news of his conquest reached the ears of neighboring tribes. The people of Gibeon formed a plan to deceive Joshua. They sent a delegation arrayed in tattered clothing and carrying moldy bread and announced to Joshua that they were a tribe from a great distance and had come to make an alliance with him. Joshua and the elders (his team) made an alliance with these clever people. But he forgot the most important ingredient: he did not consult God. When Joshua discovered the deceit, God informed him that these people would be a thorn in his side forevermore (Josh. 9). The Israelis and the Palestinians are still at odds. God could have revealed this trap to Joshua as God today can reveal defects in our plan. When we leave God out, we are certain to make crucial mistakes.

Make a Plan

When the armies of Alexander the Great led by Zenophan crossed the Persian Gulf and attacked the Persian Empire, they had fewer than 25,000 well-disciplined soldiers. They were met by 3 million unorganized Persian rabble. The 25,000 Greek soldiers easily defeated the 3 million Persians. Why? The Greeks had a plan. The Persians had the desire to defend their homeland, but they lacked a plan. They had little discipline and poor leadership, so they were easily defeated.

If a person starts to build a house without a blueprint, that house will very likely become a monstrosity. It will probably not stand up under the fierce storms of life either. Even a master builder who has built thousands of homes needs a blueprint.

Suppose I sit down in front of a piano and begin banging on the keys. How long would it be before I learned how to play? I probably never would. Learning to play the piano, like learning to do anything, requires system, order, and following a plan. System, order, and a plan were put into this universe at creation. System and order and a plan are what we need to accomplish anything worthwhile.

Now that you have your team together and you are in the process of making your plan, keep in mind the Dale Carnegie questions we established in chapters 7 and 8:

- What is the problem?
- What are the causes of the problem?
- What are some possible solutions and alternatives?
- What is the best possible solution at this moment?
- What is the plan of action to put the best possible solution to work?

Clearly detail your plan step by step, point by point. And don't let your team divert you from this plan onto another idea until your plan is complete.

Practice Your Strategy

Now it is time to practice your strategy. The army does this during war games. They divide into teams, maneuver, capture prisoners, and act as if a real war were taking place. The person who is well prepared will be more apt to win the war and solve the problem. One learns best how to respond with practice.

Often people come into my office bitter and resentful. Some couples can't be in each other's presence for five minutes without assaultive verbal barrages. We practice better ways of responding to the problems of marital life and thus help them learn how to be more compatible. I teach them how to communicate without fighting. Sometimes we role play, with me playing the part of the husband or the wife. We practice the rules of good communication over and over in these sessions until they learn how to fight fair and respond lovingly. We do the same thing in group therapy. We practice communication with a neutral party until the person becomes skilled enough to face the real thing.

One day I listened to a couple talk to each other as follows:

He: "You never show me affection anymore."

She: "You always insult me and hurt my feelings."

Me: "Both of you are using absolute words like *never* and *always*. Those words are not true. Say the same thing now without using never or always."

He: "Sometimes you are cold."

She: "Sometimes you talk rough and hurt my feelings."

Me: "That's better. Now continue talking and let's see what you say."

She: "I can't love a person who swears at me."

He: "Who wouldn't swear at a person who gripes and complains all the time?"

Me: "Both of you are speaking in terms of what you can't help instead of what you can do. Let's rephrase your sentence and practice it."

She: "It makes me very upset when you swear."

He: "I have difficulty controlling my anger when you are sarcastic and your words are biting."

Me: "I want you both to notice that when you rephrase your language in terms of the truth and with more gentleness of spirit, it does not call for such a serious response."

Too many people try to solve the most crucial problems without any experience or any practice of strategy. In order to be problem-solvers, we need to make time to practice our plan.

In the art of solving problems, practicing strategy is a very important step. When we practice our actions ahead of time, we can then work on perfecting our actions and greatly decrease the possibility of failure. Too many people try to solve the most crucial problems without any experience or any practice of strategy. In order to be problem-solvers, we need to make time to practice our plan.

Don't be afraid to review and practice anything you want to do well. The greatest musicians in the world spend hours a day perfecting their technique. You are faced with a life-changing problem. It's worth a few minutes to practice your strategy. Practicing your strategy builds self-confidence. If you are hesitant or fearful, the best possible course of action is to practice what you're going to say or do, step by step. Then, when the time comes for the real action, you will know exactly what to say and do, and those around you will sense your self-confidence. A calm, unhurried gait and a friendly, warm manner show faith in yourself and faith in your plan.

In Dr. Sidney Lecker's book, *The Natural Ways to Stress Control*, he tells of the time when he was preparing for his pilot's license and mentally conjured up possible scenarios of what he would do if various things went wrong on the instrument panel. During one of his final lessons, his instructor said, "What would it be like to land with a malfunction of your landing lights?" as he switched them off. Trembling, Sidney landed on a pitch black runway successfully. One evening while he was flying solo, that very problem *did* happen. Sidney was able to keep calm because he had practiced mentally what he would do in case of that emergency. Positive rehearsal helps a person find positive solutions in a crisis situation.

Motivational speaker and author Denis Waitley also recommends that we practice our strategy. He says when we practice what we will do in emergency situations, our unconscious automatically takes over and we are able to face the problems of life with a clear head. Denis worked with NASA astronauts and observed that they practice and practice their strategy so that they will not panic when a real emergency arises. Denis gives several examples of prisoners of war he has interviewed who practiced hundreds of times in their minds each swing on their favorite golf course. When a particular POW was finally free to play on that golf course, he played his best game ever. Why? Because he had practiced those shots in his mind hundreds of times in prison camp.

So, as you practice your strategy, you too will be prepared for whatever happens in the course of life.

Now let's take a look at how the open door of organizing works in actual practice. Several times a year I invite seven or eight good friends whose opinion I respect to be on my problem-solving team. I tell them in advance that I need their help to solve some difficult problems in my life. I promise them that I will be available when *they* need help in solving problems. It is not necessary, but I invite my group to dinner. After the meal, while we are still around the table, I call the meeting to order with a prayer and proceed immediately to present my problem. I ask them to brainstorm and bring to light any suggestion no matter how far-out. Sometimes I respond to their suggestions by explaining some details of the problem. I go around the table and encourage every person to participate. Our evening meal starts promptly at 6:00; our discussion starts at 7:00. Whether or not the problem has been solved, the discussion part of the meeting closes at 9:00. I make it a policy to state clearly my problem and not to interrupt as they reach for a solution.

The discussion of the problem often ends in just that—a discussion—unless you add the third step, practicing your strategy. Many problems will lend themselves to positive rehearsal. So don't be afraid to try it, even in front of your team if you feel comfortable with them.

But sometimes practicing my strategy is not necessary. Some solutions to problems just don't require practice. If the solution to my problem is to buy a new car, I certainly don't need to practice that. But if the solution to the problem is to dismiss an employee, in my case, I would find it helpful to set up a role-playing situation in which I practiced the proper way to do this difficult task. Maybe my team could give me pointers on how to do this more effectively.

So, practicing your strategy can take two forms: it can consist of just going over the solution until you have it clearly in mind, or it can consist of sitting your group down and practicing doing what you and the team have decided to do. Your chances of success are infinitely greater if you take the time to practice your strategy.

Last Friday night I called a meeting of the officers of the Sunday School class I teach. I presented them with the problem: "Our Sunday School class is not growing." We discussed many causes and causes of the causes. Then we arrived at a number of possible solutions. One of the solutions was to make the people feel more at home in the Sunday School class by using their names, both in making announcements and in saying prayers for them. I suggested we start by calling the people by name in our officers group. I was amazed to discover some of the people didn't know the names of the people there. So we had a practice session in which we prayed for each other by name. Each person went around the room calling the other people by name. We decided to show the class what we were doing in order to encourage them to use people's names. In this case, practicing our strategy was an absolute necessity to inaugurate the solution in the class.

When you practice your strategy, you are one step closer to solving the "elephant-sized" problems of life.

Summary

When the problems are severe, and they can't be solved by defining and opting, we pull out the bigger guns and organize for a larger war.

In the open door of organizing, we follow three steps:

- ■ Step 1: We form a team. In order to solve big problems in this world, we need the advice, emotional strength, and camaraderie of a team consisting of God, others, and ourselves.

- Step 2: We make a plan. We write down a systematic way of approaching our problem with our team's competent advice and support.

- Step 3: We practice our strategy. We take the time to go over our plan and smooth over the rough places so that when the time comes for action, we will have a sound platform to stand on. When we practice our strategy, we gain confidence in the plan and faith in our ability to succeed. And that self-confidence makes us a positive, determined winner that people recognize as such.

Organizing is an open door to problem-solving that helps immeasurably to insure the success of our plans.

Learning

The "Open Door of Learning" is divided into three parts. First enact your plan. If the plan works, hallelujah! You need go no further. If the plan doesn't work, then you need to quickly take the next step—accept your defeat. Don't continue to dwell on a plan that didn't work.

After accepting your defeat, the third step is relatively easy: learn from your defeat. You must have feedback when you miss the target of life. Go back to your team and discuss why your plan failed and change it a bit. A familiar proverb says, "Those who forget the past are doomed to repeat it." Don't repeat your errors. Take a look at them and learn from them.

Enact Your Plan

Chapter 8 talked about opting to take action after choosing a solution. This step of enacting your plan is a bit more complex. It means to take action on a *formulated* plan. To formulate plans and not take action can be a debilitating experience. Procrastination is the thief of time. The proper moment to act comes upon us, and we must take advantage of that moment.

There is a terrible disease that afflicts our age. We call it "Paralysis of Analysis." We spend so much time analyzing a problem that analysis becomes a substitute for action.

There is a terrible disease that afflicts our age. We call it "Paralysis of Analysis." We spend so much time analyzing a problem that analysis becomes a substitute for action. There comes a time when we must enact our plan or lose the war.

I have several clients who are involved in long-term psychotherapy. We never can solve their problems because they are unable to take the steps necessary to enact their plan. We reached a conclusion eight years ago that the solution to one young man's problems was to go back to college long enough to find a major interest, to train himself in that major interest, and in the process he would find meaning in life and possibly the girlfriend he was looking for. Eight years of procrastination, eight years of asking, "What should I do?" and eight years of pining for a girlfriend. I still tell him, "It's not too late," but I wonder if eight years from now he will still be putting off enacting the plan that could change his life. How tragic.

Many people have the problem of learning to conserve their strength for the major issue. They often put their strength into minor problems and have no strength left for the really important issues. Enacting your plan requires powerful energy sources to launch the solution. When a person flays the air and expends his energy, he has no strength left to solve the major problems of life.

I counseled a medical doctor who got so caught up in his own emotionality that he failed to solve his major problem of winning back his wife's love. In our sessions we enacted a plan for him to court his wife, woo her back, and reschedule his time to include her and the children in his daily life. We practiced what he was to say and do. When the time came for him to enact the plan, he abandoned all reason, dropped into a subjective emotional state and berated her vigorously for not understanding the great priority: his practice came first.

When the couple later divorced, I wondered what would have happened if he had actually *enacted his plan* and not gotten sidetracked in attacking, blaming, and projecting. He discovered to his dismay that he spent more time courting a new woman than it would have taken to enact his original plan of wooing back his wife. How fruitless it is to enact a plan in the calm, clear light of reason and then abandon it for an emotional tirade.

Accept Defeat and Move Forward

The reason many people do not enact their plan is their fear of failure. In this chapter you are learning the best way to deal with failure is to accept the defeat, learn what you did wrong, and enact another plan.

If we do not enact our plan, we will not ever know if it works. If our plan does not work, we must be able to accept defeat and move forward. Some people find it impossible to think that they could be wrong, so they are constantly defending themselves, constantly making excuses, or constantly being devastated by the failure of a plan. Life is like a football game. Our team can make a game plan and practice our strategy many times. Then, during the game, we form a huddle, enact the plan, call the signals, and still get thrown for a ten-yard loss. We teach our team to quickly accept defeat, learn from their mistakes, make another plan, and try again.

People who really don't want to solve the problem make all sorts of excuses and rationalizations. People who honestly want to solve the problem accept the defeat of a battle in order that they might try again to win the war. One of the most difficult obstacles to problem-solving comes from the perfectionist who absolutely insists on winning every battle or he won't play. If a quarterback threw a temper tantrum and stomped off the field the first time he lost yardage or failed to complete a pass, that would be the end of the game for him.

Every significant step of progress is made by stumbling a thousand times. You accept your losses and defeats. You learn from them. You make another plan and try again. It doesn't make any difference how many times you get thrown for a loss. You still come back with another plan to get around the opposition.

Every significant step of progress is made by stumbling a thousand times. You accept your losses and defeats. You learn from them. You make another plan and try again. It doesn't make any difference how many times you get thrown for a loss. You still come back with another plan to get around the opposition.

Writer Kenneth Hildebrand tells of a husband and wife who learned their teenage son was going blind. All their friends felt deep sorrow for the boy and his family. The boy's father explained, "It seems we have three choices. We can curse life for doing this to us and look for some way to express our grief and rage. We can grit our teeth and endure it. Or we can *accept it and move forward.* The first alternative is useless. The second is sterile and exhausting. The third is the only way" [*Los Angeles Times*].

When we learn to accept the experiences life throws at us as challenges, then we can learn to win in the game of life. We yield to situations we are powerless to change. When we are willing to stop fighting against the inevitable, we can free ourselves from the stress that kills. Harsh experiences that lead to defeat sometimes come upon us. To ignore defeat does not make it go away. To pretend it does not exist will not lighten our load.

When we accept defeat and move forward with courage, we are choosing to stay on the path of success.

There comes a time when we give ourselves to the situation *as it is* and see what we can do about remodeling it. To accept life and its inevitable defeats and still move forward is the only creative way.

To accept defeat doesn't mean to fold our hands in our laps and lift pious glances to heaven, feeling martyred. Acceptance is something altogether different. Acceptance is Michelangelo on his way to the marble quarry, believing that if he could find the right block of stone he could create a masterpiece. Upon arriving, all that was left was one jagged, irregular piece of marble. After studying it, he decided to accept the discarded, misshapen rock. From that ugly fragment, Michelangelo produced one of the best-loved pieces of art in the world, his *Boy David*.

He later said, "Its outline was dictated by the imperfections of the block I worked with—the bend of the head, the twist of the body, the arm holding the sling. They were all there in that jagged piece of rock."

In marriage counseling, I teach people how to confront each other fairly. One of the rules is to acknowledge when the other person has made a point. If we can't acknowledge that our opponent has landed a blow, thrown us for a loss, or succeeded in winning, then we will never truly be able to accept victory when it comes to us. When we are tagged and our opponent says, "I've got you," and we immediately throw up a childish defense mechanism with the response, "No you didn't, you didn't get me," we accomplish nothing whatsoever but to interject lies into the process of problem-solving.

Suppose that researchers trying to find a cure for cancer said, "I found it, I found it," when they hadn't. What would it profit? All they would do is defeat themselves. Not only that, but if they finally did find a cure, no one would believe them.

Some people accept defeat, then hang their heads in shame and stop trying. It seems to me the only shame is in the stopping. When we accept defeat and move forward with courage, we are choosing to stay on the path of success.

Learn from Your Defeat

A veteran of the war in Korea told me the following story. The American troops had invaded North Korea when China decided to enter the war. Hundreds of thousands of Chinese troops poured across the border, and the American forces were pushed back by this new threat. My friend was positioned on a hillside that had the valley in front of them zeroed in with 50-caliber machine guns and 75-millimeter cannons and mortars. The Chinese troops advanced across that valley, but from their invincible position the American troops mowed them down. The Chinese had only one strategy and that was to overpower the enemy with multitudes of manpower. My soldier friend said, "We killed them by the thousands and they still kept coming, climbing over their dead comrades. So we kept firing." That day broke the back of the invaders because they were unable to learn from their mistake. They were unable to change their plan. They seemed unable to do anything but forge directly ahead, beating their wings against the windowpane.

Sometimes our plans will not work. The enemy has us zeroed in. We must change our strategy or die. We must learn from our defeat or we are destined to be as dumb as the bee against the windowpane.

There is an inherent obstacle to learning from our defeat. The obstacle is the peculiar propensity of the human to believe in long shots. If someone goes to Las Vegas to gamble, the odds are against him. The house advantage is built into the system. But sometimes people win and win big. Because of this remote chance of winning, people often refuse to learn from defeat.

In a recent lottery the odds were figured at one chance in 25 million of winning the prize. Yet 25 million people took that chance. If a woman takes drugs, she is likely to get caught and ruin her life. Yet, some people don't get caught. If a person drinks too much, he is likely to become an alcoholic. Yet some people don't become alcoholics. The faster we drive our cars, the more likely we are to have automobile accidents. Yet, some people drive with no thought whatsoever of the odds catching up with them.

It is really difficult to learn from our defeats because of mathematical odds. There is no such thing as 100 percent certainty that any method will or will not work. If you find that your method of operation consistently does not succeed, you may need to try another method. Perhaps a conference with your team is needed to re-evaluate.

As a child I learned this saying, "I keep six honest serving men. They taught me all I knew: 'what' and 'when' and 'where' and 'how' and 'why' and 'who.'" Analyze a plan in light of these six ideas. What if I form a brilliant team, make an exciting plan, and practice my strategy diligently? Then I enact my plan. Woe of woes—it fails, and I accept the fact that I have been defeated. What do I do? I pick up that defeated plan and examine it in terms of:

1. *What* went wrong?
2. *When* did it go wrong?
3. *Where* are the weak points?
4. *How* can we change it?
5. *Why* are we making these changes?
6. *Who* is going to carry the ball this time?

With this quick analysis, I rapidly gain some feedback on where the plan went wrong and how I'm going to do it differently. I have to confess that I am sometimes a slow learner. I am amazed at how many times I have battered my head against the same obvious windowpane. There was a period in my life when I experienced so many repetitive failures that I thought I was a loser and that God must have it in for me. But then I had a "Eureka" experience. The reason I consistently failed was because I did not use that technique that brought humans out of the cave and into the light of day. That technique is the ability to translate the spoken word into writing.

In order to learn from defeat, a person needs to *write* his or her mistakes down. I used to say, "Well, I won't do *that* again." Lo and behold, five minutes after the words left my mouth, I was doing it again, that same stupid error. In order for me to learn from my defeats, I discovered I had to write my errors down in a systematic way. Then, when I made a new plan, it was easy to be sure that the same error didn't crop up again.

So when we learn from our defeat, we become flexible; we're able to change that part of our plan that isn't working. We call a conference with our team and write down answers to the six big questions of what, when, where, how, why, and who. Systematically, we revise our strategy and learn from our defeat.

Summary

In the open door of learning, you are encouraged to forge ahead toward success until your problem is solved. The first step was to enact your plan. If, after forming a team, making a plan, and practicing your strategy, the plan still fails, then you need to move to the second step: accept defeat and move forward. To curse your fate is useless. If you decide to endure failure, then you are settling to live life at a lower level. To accept defeat and move forward is the only creative way. Be a Michelangelo, not a General Meade.

The last step is to learn from your defeat. When you and your team get together and write down the reasons for failure and systematically change your plans and revise your strategy, then you are learning from your defeat.

You form a team, make a plan, practice your strategy, then enact your plan in a real-life situation. You may lose, but you accept it, learn from it, and try again with another plan. The number of defeats doesn't matter. You will meet the opposition with another plan. Why? Because you are a problem-solver. You practice the secret of learning from your defeat and you are confident of success as you pass through the next portal: the open door of persevering.

Persevering

To persevere when you've tried your hardest many times and failed takes real self-discipline and great determination. To "keep on keeping on" until the sweet smell of success is yours is to say to yourself, "With every defeat, I learn something new. I know how *not* to fail next time." Say with a French philosopher, "In every way, every day, I'm getting better and better."

"The Open Door of Persevering" builds real character. It has three steps: condition yourself, make another plan, and try again.

Step 1: Condition Yourself

What if we make a plan and it fails? Then we make another plan and it fails? What are we to do? We are to persevere, make another plan, and try again.

When we are trying to solve a problem and we meet with defeat, the first thing we do is *take a good look*. Why did the plan fail? We go through a mental checklist to see if we were prepared to solve the problem. The secret to the open door of persevering is to prepare ourselves for another try at solving the problem by conditioning ourselves and rethinking what went wrong.

I begin by asking myself questions in several areas.

Area 1: Mental Attitude

Do I have a good mental attitude? Do I have faith in God, people, and myself? Do I believe in my plan? Was I really ready?

One day a man who claimed he was addicted to food came into my office. He said he had tried every diet known to man, but nothing would work for him. Basically, I did not believe that was true. When people are over-weight, they have usually eaten more food than their level of physical activity needs, or they have eaten food with too much fat and sugar. All a person generally needs to do is:

1. increase the level of exercise,
2. decrease the amount of food intake,
3. cut down on fat and sugar, and
4. eat plenty of fruit, vegetables, and grains.

However, my client believed he was addicted to high-calorie foods and could not reduce food intake or increase exercise. My job was not to give him a new diet but to help change his mental attitude. When he believed he could not solve the problem, then he couldn't. When he believed he could solve the problem, then he could.

Faith is a mental attitude that is a prerequisite to problem-solving. The "God and I can do it" attitude is undefeatable in problem-solving. A change of attitude enabled my client to change his weight.

Area 2: Physical Health

Am I taking care of myself? Am I getting enough rest to allow my coping mechanisms to be "on top?" Am I allowing stress to get to me? Did I put too little or too much energy into the plan?

Some people seem to think they are immune to the laws of good health. They believe they can eat endless amounts of junk food, get too little rest and exercise, ingest toxic substances, and still be well.

When we ingest bad food and practice poor health habits, we will suffer the consequences. There are no exceptions. Some problems are very difficult and require our total strength. If we have dissipated our strength through bad health habits, we will not have the energy to solve our problems. There are no exceptions.

Area 3: Team Evaluation

Did my team do a good job? Maybe I could choose some new members for my team and get some new ideas. Maybe I didn't communicate closely enough with my team. Did I try their best suggestions? Or did I go ahead and do what I wanted to do, regardless of their counsel? Did my team use mental, spiritual, physical, and emotional energy to back me up? If not, why?

Review the team members' suggestions. Call another meeting. Inspire your team to come up with some new answers or ask them to help you inaugurate the old ones.

Area 4: Goals

Did I make realistic goals? Or did I expect too much from people, including myself? Considering my polio handicap and my age, if I had the goal of becoming a quarterback for the Los Angeles Rams, that would be unrealistic. No matter how much I tried and opted and organized and learned and persevered, I couldn't reach that goal because it is unrealistic. Thankfully, my goal was to become a pastor, a goal that I *could* reach.

A woman once said to me, "I don't think I can make it in my marriage." I said to her, "Why not?" She replied, "I have thought about it for a long time. I know I expect too much from my husband, but there is no way I can tolerate him not giving his all to me." I said to her, "I think there is a way. Have you considered setting some goals for yourself, getting some more education and becoming a real person in your own right, one who doesn't need to depend 100 percent on your husband?"

Happily, the woman reset her goals, became a therapist and was able to stay with her husband because she could accept what he had to offer. We always expect more from others than they can deliver if we haven't anything to do but depend upon them. We should periodically rethink whether or not we have set realistic goals.

Area 5: Proper Training

Did I allow myself time to get proper training before diving headlong into my solution? Did I do my homework? Did I study to anticipate the pitfalls? Did I research the field?

There can be no substitute for learning, for training, for preparing ourselves to solve a problem by gaining knowledge in the field. Not long ago a dear friend contracted cancer of the adenoids, a very unusual and fatal disease. At first, Paul was devastated by this terrible event. He no longer could perform adequately in his job or in his home. I challenged him to find out all he could about his adenoid cystic carcinoma. He became very involved in researching at the University of California, Irvine, medical library. According to the doctor, Paul was going to die within a year. Paul is still alive after eight years. One explanation is that he became so deeply involved in training himself to become an expert in this type of cancer that the training itself gave him respite.

In any case, there is no substitute for training, knowledge, and learning in the field of your problem.

Area 6: Decisiveness

Was my willingness to act coupled with the ability to take a chance, or was I waiting for that perfectly calm sea that never came? Remember General Meade who had the opportunity to stop General Lee and hence shorten the Civil War. Was I like General Meade, who hesitated and lost? Did I pass up the opportune time? How can I be ready next time?

There is a time to act and there is a time to refrain from acting. Decisiveness balances itself delicately. Sometimes we can be sure that now is the hour of decision; but usually the decisive person takes some risk. Those who fall prey to uncertainty will usually miss the boat.

The decisive person takes some risk. Those who fall prey to uncertainty will usually miss the boat.

For years I have worked with a young man who claims that all he wants from life is a girlfriend whom he can love and marry and live with happily ever after. But when the time comes to ask a girl for a date, he never has the courage to do so. He can never be decisive and take a risk. He is always afraid of being rejected, and life's great dream is passing him by because he can't take the risk of decisiveness.

After I have checked the six areas to see if I was prepared, I usually find a point or two where I goofed up. Maybe I didn't do my homework and know the facts well enough beforehand. Or maybe I allowed the stress of other pressing problems to affect me physically, or I didn't act when the time was ripe.

When we find ourselves faced with failure and it is necessary to make another plan, we need to spend a little time in preparing ourselves.

In the process of persevering and conditioning ourselves to make another plan and try again, we also need to remember to condition *others* involved in our plan and help get them ready. When we fill the air with our inspiration for another go at it, our helpers pick up on it and are also inspired.

Step 2: Make Another Plan

In the 1950s and 1960s, I taught the Dale Carnegie Course in the Los Angeles area. My mother was a successful real estate broker in Spokane, Washington. Out of a sense of loyalty to me, Mother decided to take the Dale Carnegie Course. She said, "Son, I'm afraid to take your course, but I suppose I should because most successful people take it."

"Mother, why are you afraid to take the course?"

"Because I'm an older woman, and I have become a success. I'm afraid that if I learn how to be a success, I might not be one anymore."

"Mother, that's crazy," I said, "but you do have a point. You are a financial and personal success under very difficult circumstances. Why change a method that works?"

My point is that if your plan works, why change it, even if someone claims to have a better idea? You can't beat success.

But if your plan *doesn't* work, it makes good sense to consider making another plan. It's dumb to continue in the same old way when the same old way doesn't bring the desired results.

If we are talking about value systems, that's another ball game. We may have to stand firm with our plan even if we know that our plan will meet with great opposition. It's like a man insisting that his car will run on water. He pours water in the gas tank, but the car doesn't budge out of the driveway. Sooner or later he has to face the fact that cars run on gasoline, not water. He might say, "But look how convenient it is to use water. I just stick the hose in the tank. And water's a lot cheaper than gasoline. Water *ought* to work!" "Ought to's" and "should be's" and "must be's" can be wonderful idealism, but idealism doesn't solve problems. Pragmatism does. We must deal with *what is.*

Persistence is a good trait when you're on the right track, but if you're on the wrong track, all the persistence in the world won't change the outcome.

No matter how much we want our car to run on water, it won't cooperate. Why? Because we are fighting against the nature of things. Persistence is a good trait when you're on the right track, but if you're on the wrong track, all the persistence in the world won't change the outcome.

Sometimes we have to make another plan, not because we did something wrong, but because that's the way of life. The farmer plants his crop, tends it all summer, and the week before harvest the boll weevils eat it up. You lose for no good reason. It's part of the fabric of life to lose sometimes. If the farmer doesn't plant his crop, one thing is guaranteed: no crop.

Often parents who are having problems with their children come to me for counseling. They tell me all the good things they do and the bad things the child does. No matter what the parents do, the child acts this bad way. I present them with another plan that might work. They insist that their way of dealing with the child must work, and they want me to do something to the child so that their bad method will get good results. They want to change the result without changing the cause. Life just doesn't work that way. When we give up pride or whatever is hindering us and change the plan to something that has a better chance of working, then we can see successful results.

In my counseling practice I always present people with alternatives—different ways of looking at things, different ways of coping and solving problems. Absolutists and legalists often believe there is only one way to do anything, but those who are skilled problem-solvers know that there are many ways to climb a mountain.

To persevere and make another plan requires discipline and a faith that says, "Yes, there is another way, and I'm going to keep on until I find it."

To persevere and make another plan requires discipline and a faith that says, "Yes, there is another way, and I'm going to keep on until I find it."

Step 3: Try Again

After you have adjusted your plan, you have the opportunity to try the plan again. Many problems do not lend themselves to simple solutions. When a problem is too big, we must divide it into smaller ones that will lend themselves to a ready solution and larger ones that require more thinking.

Let's say you are assigned the task of excavating a hillside. In one spot the hill lends itself to a shovel. In another place, you may need to use a pick. In some areas, you might need a bulldozer, and sometimes the only solution is a stick of dynamite. Different solutions are necessary for different circumstances. Sometimes we need to attack the problem from several directions.

The children's story of "The Little Engine that Could" is a real inspiration to me. The little engine tried and tried to get over the hill with an attitude of faith saying, "I think I can, I think I can." Faith turns the tide at a critical point of problem-solving. To try again means that you have faith. To give up is the opposite of having faith. It means giving in to your fears. Myriads of people have failed because they thought they couldn't do it. But some have succeeded in the same task with the same or less ability simply because they said, "I think I can."

Determined and disciplined people are the winners, the problem-solvers of life.

There is an attraction at Palm Springs, California, that has inspired me to push a little harder in my personal battles of life. One man had a vision of building a monumental tramway system from the desert floor to the top of a huge mountain. He wanted to share with others the beauty he had found on "his mountain." Against insurmountable odds and numerous scoffers who said it couldn't be done, he raised the money, hired the technicians from Switzerland, found ways to transport the heavy equipment up sheer granite walls, paid the engineers and workers, raised more money, built a chalet on top for cross-country skiers, and saw his dream come true.

Because one man believed in himself and persevered, trying again and again, nature and God and people cooperated with him, and he succeeded. Determination and self-discipline is learned mainly through experience. Determined and disciplined people are the winners, the problem-solvers of life.

The nature of problems requires that we ask for help, form a plan, and try various solutions until we are successful. That's what Thomas Edison did while trying to invent an electric light. After five years of failure, a helper said to him, "You've made no progress." Edison replied, "Yes, I have. I now know 2,000 ways how not to make an electric light." A part of the mechanism of solving problems is to keep on trying until you find your way out of the maze. "Knock, and it shall be opened unto you" (Matt. 7:7, KJV).

On television I watched the story of a man who is determined to find Bigfoot. Every summer the same man goes into the Pacific Northwest to look for Bigfoot, and every year he has failed to find scientific proof of Bigfoot's existence. That man said "Yep, I'm gonna go again next summer." If Bigfoot does exist, there's a good chance he will be the one to find him because he is practicing the rule of trying again.

Summary

The open door of persevering is a real character-building door. Determination and discipline can only be developed through perseverance. To *condition yourself* you ask, "Do I have a good mental attitude? Do I have faith in myself? Do I believe in my plan? Am I doing all I can to keep myself healthy and alert? Did I form a good team? Did I try their best suggestions? Did I set realistic goals? Did I expect too much of others? Did I get the proper training? Did I research the field? Did I decisively act when the proper time came?"

After completing your mental checklist, the next step is to *make another plan.* If the car won't run on water, then try gasoline. If your ought-to-be's and should-be's are failing, then find out *what is* and change your plan.

The last step through the open door of persevering is to *try again.* To try again means to have faith in your team, your God, and yourself.

So, if your plan doesn't work, learn from your defeat, condition yourself, make another plan and make another and make another plan. Keep making plans and trying until you find a plan that works.

Motivating

Someone asked me, "In solving problems, why doesn't motivation come first?" The answer is that it does come first, but also second, third, fourth, fifth, sixth, etc. I've placed "The Open Door of Motivating" as one of the last so that if you happen to fail this time, you can start the whole process over again—motivated.

There are three basic ways of motivating a person to solve the problems of life. The first is emotional: harness emotional energy and direct that energy toward our goals. The second is cognitive: direct our mental energy toward the achievement of a solution. The third is behavioral: glory in our victory, to reward ourselves when we achieve our goal so we will be motivated to meet the next challenge.

The combination of emotional, mental, and behavioral forces generates a fourth motivational dynamic—a spiritual force that shows great love for our fellow humans and a desire to help others in need.

Step 1: Harness Emotional Energy

The engineering law of entropy states, "As the heat of the body rises, so the energy available for work diminishes." Thus if you get emotionally upset, you will have less ability to solve problems.

Whenever we find ourselves getting emotionally upset and we are in the process of solving a problem, we have two ways to go: stop trying to solve the problem, or direct our emotional energy into solving the problem. Emotional energy backed by intelligence and directed toward the problem is one of the greatest forces on earth.

Jesus is a perfect example of one who harnessed His emotional energy. He spent three and a half years teaching, preaching, and healing in the obscure villages of Palestine. Most of His great truths were taught in a calm and peaceful way.

But when Jesus spent a day on a cross, passionate and emotional words came from deep within Him such as, "My God, my God, why hast thou forsaken me?" (Matt. 27:46, KJV). Of course, God had not forsaken Him except for the brief moment the sins of the world were laid upon Him. Jesus continued, "Into thy hands I commend my spirit" (Luke 23:46, KJV), and He died with a loud cry.

Nothing on earth is more emotional than the cross of Jesus Christ. Out of His emotional death on the cross came the resurrection and devout followers who changed the world.

One problem with the control of emotions is that some people imagine that emotions come upon us from outside stimuli and automatically generate themselves. They are confusing the idea of emotional spontaneity with the reflex phenomenon. For example, if someone in a scary mask were to suddenly run up to me while I was preoccupied with something else, I would probably jump. That's the startle reflex. The cerebral cortex is slower than the startle reaction. So, the person who put his masked face next to mine and said, "Boo," made me jump. But after I have time to consider what happened, I will laugh.

At the proper stimulus, emotions are generated from the brain stem, sometimes as quickly as the startle reflex. But the cerebral cortex that thinks things out can very quickly take control. So, if we are slapped, we may emit a shout or cry, a spontaneous startle reflex. Then, when our best friend says, "I'm sorry. It was an accident. Forgive me," we quickly gain control of the mounting emotional tide.

That's my point. The cognitive power of the human mind is more powerful than its emotions. Emotions do not have to run rampant. Emotions are made to assist the reasoning processes.

I have developed a little technique I call "generation" that helps me get to work. What I do is force a feeling—anger for instance—to surface in my mind. Then I quickly transform it into creativity. This technique helps me generate some good ideas for writing. Let's look at how generation works.

Emotions do not have to be an accidental, capricious, impulsive waste of time. You can put them to work by harnessing your emotional energy and using that energy to solve problems.

We are reaching for a juicy, red apple on the branch of a tree . . . just out of reach. If we can get our adrenaline flowing, we'll be able to jump higher and get the apple. So, if out of frustration, I get angry, the emotional force of anger backs up my jump and I can reach the apple. That's natural.

I also have learned to mentally generate a feeling similar to that of anger, discharge the adrenals, and use that extra force in a creative way. That's also natural.

Emotions do not have to be an accidental, capricious, impulsive waste of time. You can put them to work by harnessing your emotional energy and using that energy to solve problems.

Step 2: Direct Mental Energy

All the magnificent accomplishments of humankind have been achieved mainly through the proper use of brain power. You can use your brain to solve problems, and I've suggested a number of techniques. But you can also use your brain to motivate yourself.

In my clinic we had a galvanic skin response machine that measured the electrical impulses of the sweat glands. I noticed a very interesting phenomenon: those people who have large amounts of electrical energy also have large amounts of enthusiasm and motivation.

With training and mental effort, a person who has low electrical energy levels can speed up the electricity-producing efforts of the neurons. As I connected people to the galvanic skin response machine, I asked them to think of certain stimulating ideas, and they began to produce more electricity. My conclusion is that the human brain can be influenced by what we call the human will or self-determination to make things better.

We can decide that we are going to be more enthusiastic, more motivated, more excited, or more involved and our brain will rise to meet the demand. With my own eyes I have seen people will themselves to live when medically the odds were against them. I have also seen slightly ill patients give up and die. People become despondent, discouraged, unhappy, and unwilling to go on. They turn to the command center and sometimes unconsciously issue an order of death, which is obeyed by the brain. I personally believe there is a positive correlation between many terminal illnesses and people developing a "give-up-itis" type personality syndrome.

I talked one day with a man in the Veteran's Hospital in Long Beach, California. He had stepped on a land mine in Viet Nam and both legs were blown off. He was filled with discouragement. He told me, "Doctor Diehm, I just don't want to live without my legs." So he turned away from life and methodically gave up. He could have been fitted with artificial legs, but he died because he gave up his will to live.

Another nineteen-year-old boy I know reacted entirely differently to similar circumstances. Marty's car was smashed in an intersection, throwing his athletic body onto the busy street. His neck was broken, and he became a quadriplegic overnight. As he lay in the hospital in a steel cast, he exclaimed, "I'm going to do something worthwhile for my fellowman. I have prayed to God that I might walk again."

I interrupted, "But Marty, what if you don't?"

"Well, in that case I will just spend my life saying worthwhile things with my mouth."

With physical therapy and prayer, Marty now is sitting up in a wheelchair. Harnessing his emotional and mental energies has made it possible for Marty even to walk a little.

One man gave up his will to live and died after losing his legs. Another man lives with contentment. What makes the difference? I saw Marty turn himself on to fight back against his unfortunate circumstances. You too have this choice.

How do you direct your mental energy to motive yourself to solve problems? I have seven ideas that work for most of my clients.

Determine that you can. Determine that you can turn up the light of energy within your brain like a person turns up a rheostat on an electric light system. You *can* make the light of life shine brighter. If you don't think you can, you probably won't try, and if you don't try, you won't know.

Lift your mind positively. Use meditation, prayer, cognitive imagery, relaxation, brainstorming, creative thinking, or any technique that you can invent to find a way to get your mind and your emotions motivated. I often motivate myself by simple self-encouragement. I clap my hands and say, "Rah, rah, Bill. You can do it." I say this as I go to bed at night and as I wake up in the morning. I cheer myself on to tackle the problems of life.

Change the way you say things. One day I yelled at my assistant and hurt her feelings. Actually, I was angry at myself. (that's called projection, remember.). I began to get very negative and discouraged. I asked myself, "What good did that do?" The answer: it didn't do any good. So I made the decision: "I'm not going to do that anymore." And I am doing better.

So, mental decision-making helps me direct my mental energy. I cognitively choose to say pleasant things, then I stick to my decision. Whenever I am tempted to vent my anger on those who are not the source of my frustration, I vividly recall my mental decision and intellectually choose to let my brain, not my emotions, run the show. If I catch myself becoming short-tempered, I ignore my failure and concentrate on the goal of directing my anger in a positive way.

Change the way you act. Lead your feelings by acting like you want to feel. If you want to feel cheerful and happy, act cheerful and happy. Let your feelings follow your thoughts, your words, and your actions.

When my sons were young, I took them fishing. My youngest son, Philip, did not want to go on one fishing trip. Since there was no place to leave him, I said to him in exasperation, "You are going whether you want to or not, and you are going to fish." Philip reluctantly began to fish. He finally decided that since he had to be there anyway, he might as well act pleasantly. This attitude that Philip nurtured as a small boy has become one of the greatest strengths of his character as an adult. By the time the charter boat docked back at Long Beach Harbor, he had talked himself into actually having a good time. He even caught a prize fish. In his excitement, he showed the captain, a professional fisherman, how he baited his hook to get the catch of the day, an immense black bass.

Philip changed the way he was acting and turned a miserable day into a memorable day. I have done the same thing many times. I have found that when I make myself do what I don't want to do, I can end up really enjoying the task.

Philip changed the way he was acting and turned a miserable day into a memorable day.

If we follow our feelings, we may cause problems. If we follow our actions, we often can avert problems by changing our feelings.

Resist the opposition. Some people are amazed at opposition. They evidently have the idea that someone should spread a red carpet and toss pink carnations before them with thunderous applause as they walk down the road of life. That seldom happens. When you play a game, it makes no sense unless there is an opposing team out to get us. I've got news for you. The evil one is alive and well, and we meet his opposition everywhere we go. It is often impossible to do anything meaningful without experiencing opposition. Insecurity, anxiety, fear, and resentment desire to possess us. When you fight against them with their opposite feelings, you overcome anger with love, fear with faith, and negativism with hope. Welcome your opposition, but don't give in to it. That's what makes the game of life worthwhile.

I have found that when I make myself do what I don't want to do, I can end up really enjoying the task.

There's an old Arabian folk tale of a camel who begged his master to let him stick his nose in the tent because the night was so cold. The kindhearted master agreed. Then the camel begged for just his head, then just his neck. When morning came, the camel occupied the tent and the Arab was outside on the cold sand. When depression sticks its nose into your tent, give it a whack and make it stay outside in the desert where depression belongs. If you allow the evil one to occupy the house of your mind, he will take over and leave you dead.

Enrich your mind. Constantly use your mind in positive, creative, achieving ways. If your mind is busy and active in doing a great work, it is very seldom captured by triviality. Fill your mind with worthwhile and positive things. "Finally, brethren, whatever is true, whatever is honorable, whatever is right, whatever is pure, whatever is lovely, whatever is of good repute, if there is any excellence and if anything worthy of praise, let your mind dwell on these things" (Phil. 4:8, NASB).

There is an old saying that the evil one seeks for an empty house to occupy. (See Luke 11:24–26.) Don't let the house of your brain be empty. Read, study, learn, share, and communicate.

I have a client who chose to enrich his mind and thus solve a major problem in his life. Ralph was what I call a

HRC (Help-Rejecting Complainer). He had been in counseling with me for two full years, and there were no breakthroughs, no Eureka experiences, no insight into his presenting problem. One day, perhaps out of desperation, I brought a psychology textbook to the therapy session and read a paragraph aloud. Ralph was fascinated and he asked to borrow the book. Soon he was deeply interested in learning why people act as they do. To make a long story short, Ralph slowly changed from a HRC (Help-Rejecting Complainer) to a HAP (Help-Accepting Praiser). When he decided to enrich his mind, it helped him to become accepting instead of rejecting.

If you allow the evil one to occupy the house of your mind, he will take over and leave you dead.

Most of the problems in this world have a solution in some book. Read and study to find answers.

Develop a positive value system. Couple the motivational power of your cognitive processes with a value system. You can't truly solve any worthwhile problem in life if you do not have a moral system, something that says, "This is right and that is wrong." There is no value in solving the problems of life unless we put our marvelous brains to work on the side of good and right.

In the book *The Cross and the Switchblade*, David Wilkerson tells of his ministry to gangs in the streets of New York City. Whenever gang members met Christ and accepted Him, they dropped their switchblades of violence and picked up the cross of love. All over the world the same story is told. Accepting Jesus changes lives, and changed lives adopt a new value system. The best value system I have ever heard of is Christianity. When we accept Christ and adopt His positive value system, we solve problems.

Accepting Jesus changes lives, and changed lives adopt a new value system. The best value system I have ever heard of is Christianity. When we accept Christ and adopt His positive value system, we solve problems.

Step 3: Glory in Your Victory

The open door of motivation helps us learn to glory in our victory. When we make a touchdown, we need to be sure to reward ourselves or the inclination will be not to make a touchdown again. No cheering, and the team soon lies down on the job. Whenever you solve a problem, be excited and thrilled and complimentary that you and your team have a victory.

A pigeon can be trained to perform all kinds of tasks using positive reinforcement. For a few kernels of corn, the U.S. Coast Guard at one time had pigeons manning (or shall I say "pigeoning") their search planes. When a plane flies over an area searching for debris or survivors of a wreck, the pigeon is twenty-five times more likely than a man to sight a tiny object in a vast sea. So, rewarding the pigeon saves the lives of people who go down in the sea.

What works for pigeons works for all living species, particularly people. People do better on any job when they are rewarded. So, when you solve a problem, remember to reward yourself. When you do, you are motivated to become a better problem-solver.

In counseling, I urge people who have lost their joy of living to make a list of at least fifteen things they like to do, and then begin to do some of those things. When we reward ourselves, we return to the joy of living.

Our capitalistic system gives financial remuneration to hardworking entrepreneurs. Why does this system work so well? Because people work best when they are rewarded for their extra effort. Doing the right thing has rewards. No rewards, and soon we will have no feedback, and we may cease doing the right thing.

Here are some examples of how you can glory in your victory. If your problem is being overweight and you exercise for twenty minutes daily, you might reward yourself by watching your favorite TV show that night. If your problem is being late to work, and you are on time for a month, go buy that wallet you've been wanting. When you glory in your victory, that motivates you to achieve.

But what if your position in the game of life makes it so that you are supportive and never make that touchdown alone? Then glory in your team's victory, not just your own. When NASA landed on the moon, two men stepped out of the space capsule, but thousands of people helped make it possible. The thousands cheered as if *they* were stepping out on the surface of the moon, and in a way they were.

Also, learn how to glory in just playing the game. Whether people make a touchdown or not, they are winners when they put their *all* into the game of life. Having played a good game *is* being a winner. The linebacker will cheer and needs to cheer as much as the quarterback and the wide end receiver. If the linebacker doesn't do his job, the quarterback can't do his. Everyone on the team jumps for joy when their man makes a touchdown, even everyone on the bench.

Remember the folk tale of the little wheel in the factory. It became sad because it never got any attention. No one ever cleaned and oiled it. So the little wheel decided to stop. When the little wheel stopped, the slightly larger wheel stopped, which stopped the middle-sized wheel, which stopped the large wheel, which stopped the larger wheel, which stopped the biggest wheel of all, which stopped the factory, which threw everyone out of work, which made the little wheel know that it was really as important as the big wheel. The biggest wheel of all can't run if it's not backed up by a lot of little wheels. To keep the factory going, the little wheel, as well as the big wheel, must be rewarded.

The biggest wheel of all can't run if it's not backed up by a lot of little wheels.

If you don't take the time to reward yourself, all of the suggestions I made in this book will not work for you. Glory in your victory. Glory in the game. Glory in your supportive position. Glory as a little wheel or a big wheel. Glory forevermore.

Summary

The open door of motivating has taught us how to harness our emotional energy, how to direct our mental energy, and how to glory in our victory. In this chapter we have learned how to motivate the whole person: the emotional, the mental, and the behavioral.

How do we solve problems? We take the eternal value system given to us by God. We mix it richly with the powerful intellectual flavor of our magnificent minds. We grab the motivational forces of faith, hope, and love; direct ourselves toward a cause; then direct our emotional power. With these resources and with God's help, we can solve any problem.

Now you have the wisdom of almost fifty years of experience on how to solve problems. You are well-equipped to solve any problem life hands you. What is there left to do? Just one thing, my friend—go out there and do it!

PART 3

Through the Open Door

Taking Action

I closed chapter 12, the open door of motivating, with the idea, "You now know how to solve problems. What is there left to do? Just one thing—go out there and do it."

But the action step is not as easy as just saying, "Do it." Many people get to the place of doing it and can't do it.

I have talked to a number of intelligent people who knew the natural rules of problem-solving yet didn't solve their problems. So I have made it a habit of asking them this question: "After knowing all these techniques for problem-solving, why did you fail to solve your problem?" They usually answer, "Because I was not able to take action."

Why People Don't Take Action

After years of dialogue and watching people both succeed and fail in reaching their goals, I have pinpointed four major reasons why people don't take action when they *know* what to do. They are:

1. Lack of self-confidence.
2. The habit of procrastination.
3. Fear of failure and rejection.
4. Lack of a higher purpose.

I discovered these four reasons when I was a boy of twelve. This is how it happened. I wanted to show off for my Uncle Lee, who was my childhood hero. At a lake just outside of Aberdeen, Washington, was a raft with a diving board that was fifteen feet high. I begged Uncle Lee to take me to the lake. I wanted to show him that I could jump off that diving board. Finally, the great day came. He invited all the relatives, about twenty in all, to a picnic where brave little Billy would entertain the family by jumping off that treacherous new diving board. They all left the picnic spot and gathered by the water to watch me as I swam to the raft and pulled myself hand over hand to the top of the diving board. I scooted myself out to the edge and looked down at the water, eyes bulging. Honest—it looked like fifteen hundred feet to me, not fifteen. The more my relatives hooted and waved for me to jump, the more I clung to that board. I had *lost my self-confidence* and frankly was afraid. My heart was racing; the hairs on the back of my neck were stiff and wet with sweat. I was too embarrassed to crawl back down, but I just couldn't dive off. So I sat there procrastinating until all my relatives, even my Uncle Lee, gave up on me and walked back to the picnic area. My purpose for taking the dive had vanished. In a burst of desperation, I finally dived off, but there was no one left to applaud me. I missed the opportune moment to take action; and though I finally did act, it was too late. I never forgot the pain of that failure. Neither did I forget the four reasons why I became immobilized and unable to act when I really wanted to.

Let's look at these four reasons why people don't take action when they really want to and discover what you can do to help you take action when it is time.

Develop Self-confidence

Many people don't know that self-confidence is an ingredient that comes mainly from choice. Children naturally grow into self-confident adults through the development of competence, achievement, and praise. But it is possible for an adult who was praised a lot as a child still to have feelings of inferiority. When the adult learns that self-confidence is a choice, he or she finds that feelings of inferiority can be overcome. One can choose to become self-confident. The following steps have helped my clients build self-confidence:

Let God love you. The truly motivated problem-solvers believe that the universe is a friendly place and that God loves them. Such problem-solvers are in cooperation with life, not antagonistic to it. They believe that life is dependable, predictable, and friendly to them if they obey the rules. People who let God love them have self-confidence.

If a child is born into a home where the parents do not show adequate love and nurturing, it is difficult for that child to grow up as a positive, self-confident adult. But that deprived adult can learn how to become self-confident by taking this first and most important step of letting God love him or her.

When we let God love us, the world takes on a different glow. A colleague of mine, Dr. Gordon Farrington, explains it this way: "When I teach my clients who are suffering from lack of self-esteem to repeat this phrase over and over, day in and day out, maybe fifty times a day, the words, 'God loves me,' they begin to believe it. They begin to act as if they are loved. Then they are free to show more love to others and develop self-confidence."

Avoid negativism. In the past fifty years I have counseled almost sixty thousand people. In my observation the first and major cause of unhappiness and mental illness is negativism: the constant expression of what's wrong and why it can't be remedied. The negative person allows him or herself to become consumed by the problem. Then any solution looks hopeless. My advice is to choose to focus on what is right with the world, not on what is wrong with the world.

In Revelation 19, a frightening analogy emerges: the end of the world has come. The battle of Armageddon has begun. The angels of God have arrayed themselves on the side of Christ to engage in final battle with the angels of Satan. The Christ in magnificent robes sits on a white horse, a symbol of victory, with a sword coming out of His mouth. The symbolism strikes us that the last battle is one of words, ideas, and concepts. If the sword was in His right hand, then the battle would be physical. But the sword comes from His mouth, so the battle is verbal. Satan is fighting us with bad words, negative words, cruel and vicious concepts, destructive ideas. Christ is fighting with good words, positive words, kind and constructive concepts, fulfilling and abundant ideas.

The first and major cause of unhappiness and mental illness is negativism: the constant expression of what's wrong and why it can't be remedied. My advice is to choose to focus on what is right with the world, not on what is wrong with the world.

If people become negative in their outlook, they are on the wrong side. Their captain is on a black horse, and they won't and can't win. You can't solve problems or be self-confident if you pick up the sword of the evil one—negativism.

Talk positively to yourself. When things are not going positively, it is very difficult to talk positively. A nurse told me of a patient who came to the hospital to deliver a baby. The baby was born paralyzed from the waist down and with fluid on the brain. The nurse said to me, "How can I talk positively to myself when I run across such a horrible event?"

I recognize that there is a time for everything. There is a time to mourn, a time to cry, and a time to rejoice. "To every thing there is a season, and a time to every purpose under the heaven" (Eccles. 3:1, KJV). Bad events need to be met by appropriate sorrow and appropriate effect. The question is, how long do we stay negative in the face of negative events? The answer is: no longer than is absolutely necessary.

I have a friend, Jack Schaible, who considers the birth of his hydrocephalic brain-damaged child to be the greatest blessing of his life. The most horrible thing that ever happened is when humankind cruelly crucified the Son of God, and yet from this negative, brutal event has come the most positive program for the healing of humankind that the universe has ever known.

My point is that we should express sorrow during life's tragedies, but if we stop at that spot, life will become negative and useless. We must turn the negative into the positive by our uplifting and cheerful verbalizations. Talk to yourself as if you were a cheerleader. Never give up hope, even in the most hopeless situation. From Jesus' death on the cross came the life of resurrection. That's our foundation for hope.

Become good at something. If you have lost your way, let me remind you that we are talking about methods of building self-confidence, a self-confidence that enables a person to take action in the solving of problems. One of the steps in developing self-confidence is to become an expert in something. Notice that I say "in something." No one can become an expert in everything. But when you discipline yourself to do one thing well, you build into your system a feeling of confidence that spills over into every other aspect of life. For example, a great tennis player may be lousy at spelling. However, the self-confidence that comes from being competent in tennis neutralizes the effect of incompetence in spelling. Think of how much worse it would be to be a poor speller who was also poor at everything else.

When I went through college, I spent more time at the Ping-Pong™ table than anyone else. Even though I was physically inferior, I became so good at the game that it was rare for anyone to beat me. I gained a lot of status and self-confidence from being a good Ping-Pong™ player. What has that to do with solving problems and making decisions? When you develop self-confidence you feel good about yourself and you learn to trust yourself.

Build a system of rewards. I am constantly amazed at the number of people who have not caught on to the fact that in our country we use the capitalistic system and are motivated by rewards. A person gets paid for going to work and doing a job. Those people who do not get paid or rewarded for doing a job soon find the job not worth doing.

I can look back on my life and see some bad times, times in which I walked in the shadow of gloom and felt that life was not worthwhile. The worst time I can remember is when I awoke to the realization that I had worked for one month and had not collected a single fee for services rendered. A deep depression fell upon me. I couldn't help but feel that my counseling must indeed be poor if not a single person bothered to pay me. Since that time I have corrected my poor business practices, but I will never forget how devastating to my self-confidence it was when there were no rewards for labor.

If you want to develop self-confidence so you can be a decision-maker, you must provide yourself with a system of rewards for good and profitable behavior. Some significant other must hand out a few "good boys." Someone must take the time to encourage you with a pat on the back. The boss on occasion must increase your salary. If not, it will be difficult to continue work. Self-confidence is certainly a choice, but it is also a choice based upon the feeling of worth that comes from being rewarded for your effort.

Be around people who build you up. Everyone has heard the saying, "Evil companions corrupt good morals." And who hasn't been belabored with the story of the one bad apple that corrupts the whole barrel of good apples? Even though it is a cliche, it is true. If you choose losers for friends, you will certainly become a loser; and if you choose to remain around people who are hyper-critical and judgmental, don't be surprised to awaken as a discouraged person with lack of confidence.

I can't think of anything that can be more damaging to children than to be reared in a home where they are put down. There are two things that a child needs, and one is good roots. Good roots come from good people. Gather good people around yourself and the tree you grow will be strong and confident. Gather bad people around yourself and you will find that over-compensation for an inferiority complex will destroy most effective relationships. The second thing a child needs is self-confidence born of honest praise for what the child does well.

Balance your self-esteem. Self-esteem is thinking well of oneself, having self-respect. It is so easy to turn self-esteem into conceit by thinking too well of oneself. We are warned in the Bible, "not to think of [ourselves] more highly than [we] ought to think; but to think soberly, according as God hath dealt to every man a measure of faith" (Rom. 12:3, KJV). We are also warned that God considers us to be His children: "The Spirit Himself bears witness with our spirit that we are children of God, and if children, heirs also, heirs of God and fellow-heirs with Christ" (Rom. 8:16–17, NASB). God does not want His children to think of themselves as inferior. The task is to keep our self-esteem in balance—not too high and not too low.

Simply stated, "Don't puff yourself up, and don't deflate yourself." Everyone knows something good about themselves and probably everyone has done something for which they feel ashamed. An honest self-evaluation, listing objectively our virtues and our vices is one of the steps of Alcoholics Anonymous to gain the strength to quit drinking.

Honesty avoids such phrases as "I always," "You never," "I can't," and "You must." Extreme statements on either end of the continuum, such as telling a child, "You never do anything right," destroys the child. And statements that are gratuitously flattering make a person believe in lies. Look at yourself honestly. Get someone else's opinion to verify your strengths and your weaknesses. We need to work on our weaknesses and capitalize on our strengths. To tell a person who cannot walk because he has no legs, "Come on, you can do it; you can walk," is a cruel lie, as cruel as it is to tell a person who has the potential to walk that he can't do it.

To build honest self-confidence requires a positive look at what we do have as well as what we don't. Anything that is built on a lie is built on shaky ground.

We have reviewed seven steps to help us acquire self-confidence. The most important point to remember is that self-confidence is a choice. Whenever you feel the need for more self-confidence, make up your mind that you can have it. The self-confident person can and does make decisions and becomes a problem-solver.

Overcome the Habit of Procrastination

The second reason people don't take action is because they have developed the habit of procrastination.

First, let's define procrastination. It is the act or habit of putting things off until later—to delay or postpone. To delay or postpone with some people is a vicious habit that keeps them from making decisions. In that case, procrastination can become a defense mechanism. However, some delay in decision-making is needful. No one should make a decision until the facts necessary to make the decision have been gathered. If we decide too quickly, we become impulsive and not intelligent problem-solvers. If we procrastinate, we will lose the opportune moment for a decision.

Impulsiveness is not a problem-solver. It is merely a method to get rid of the problem quickly and hope that by some accident or act of fate the problem will be solved. Neither is procrastination a problem-solver. So, as we teach people to conquer the habit of procrastination, we must be certain that we do not overteach so that they get in the habit of making impulsive decisions. Such a habit of impulsiveness is as detrimental to problem-solving and decisiveness as is procrastination.

Make a checklist for decisiveness. My favorite word, *balance,* comes to mind. If we act too impulsively, we won't solve the problem; and if we procrastinate, we will never take action on solving the problem. Therefore, *timing* is crucial. When is the proper time to make the decision? Because I was afraid, I procrastinated and sat on that diving board until I missed a golden moment to impress my family and build my self-esteem. The proper time to act stands midway between procrastination and impulsiveness. How can I know when the right moment has come for me to act? The answer to this question has troubled men since Adam and Eve. No one has 20-20 foresight. There is a certain amount of risk in timing. The balance point is not known, but the following checklist can help us reach the moment of decisiveness.

- Ask God and listen for an answer. Many people have the faith to ask God, but few people have the faith to listen to the inner voice that answers back. I know that it is easy to use this step as a rationalization for every poor decision. Some people rather enjoy blaming God for their bad decisions. Others seem to enjoy not including God in anything. Again, the word is *balance*. If we sincerely ask God's direction and sincerely listen for His answer, I think we will make fewer mistakes.

■ If possible, ask your team of advisors. I have recommended elsewhere in this book that each person gather around him a team of advisors. We need to ask the question, "Team, we now have a pretty good idea of what we need to do to solve this problem. When is the appropriate time to enact our plan and who is going to do it?" Sometimes, as in the case of me on the diving board, no advisors are available.

■ Use your best judgment. No one wants to make a mistake. Few people want to take a chance. We all want certainty. Everyone wants to be right. But in this world, we cannot eliminate some error, the laws of probability, and the necessity of taking some risks. We have now thoroughly prepared and we have put the best of our mind and heart into the solution. We have asked God for help, and we have asked our team for advice. All the factors have been considered. We go ahead. We make the decision.

■ Have faith in the results. One of the most popular verses in the Bible is Romans 8:28, "And we know that God causes all things to work together for good to those who love God, to those who are called according to His purpose" (NASB). I have discovered that sometimes when I made a decision and it seemed to be the wrong one, it actually wasn't. Years later, when all the evidence was in, that which seemed wrong at the time was actually the right way. To avoid the habit of procrastination, I suggest deciding to have faith in your best decision.

After all these years I can look back and see that my decision to procrastinate jumping off the diving board until it was too late was the right one because it gave me an illustration for this book, and I have faith that this book will help you.

How do I break the habit of procrastination? Procrastination is habit-forming. Obviously, it is hard work to make decisions. It is also extremely risky. Therefore, it is easier not to make decisions and less fearful not to take risks. Since we know that procrastination is habit-forming, we need to use a method of breaking a bad habit. Two great men of history, William James and Benjamin Franklin, both separately worked on developing a method of breaking bad habits. Here is a brief summary of what they said:

- Write down clearly and concisely what your bad habit is.
- Determine that it is possible to cure this bad habit.
- Develop a method that you think has a chance of working.
- Put together some symbolic reminder of that particular bad habit.
- Set a day or time that you will start to work on your bad habit.
- Let nothing that exists stop you from starting the program on the day you planned.
- Don't let an exception occur to your plan for at least two weeks. It takes two weeks for a bad habit to be unlearned. Therefore, you must hold firm for that amount of time.

Now let's look at the bad habit of procrastination. I have set a goal for myself to write three pages a day on a devotional book. I have been writing on that book off and on for about five years. The reason I don't finish it is because I procrastinate writing my three pages a day. If I wish to change the situation and get into a habit of decisiveness in my writing, here's how I apply the seven steps:

- I write down the statement, "I want to write three pages a day for my devotional book."

- I will talk over with a few friends (my wife, my assistant, and the business director of our counseling clinic) to see if my time schedule will permit one-half hour a day on this new book. Can I add this time to my schedule?

- I believe that I can spend one-half hour a day reading the paper instead of my current one hour a day. I can give that extra half hour to writing this new devotional book. That is a method that has a chance of working.

- I need a symbolic reminder of my new behavior to break the bad habit. I have a tie clip that has a carving of an open book. I will determine that that tie clip will be symbolic of the one-half hour that I will spend on the new book. I will wear that tie clip every day to remind me of my one-half hour writing pledge.

- I set a date to start working on the new behavior. I determine that the first of the month will be the day that I start this program. That is two weeks from today. In the next two weeks, I will constantly remind myself of the big day coming and what I am going to do. I will set my tie clip out in a prominent place where I can see it, and on the first of the month I will wear the tie clip every day until the project is completed.

- I start the program on the prescheduled day. If I say the first is the day, nothing short of a major tragedy will stop me. I always make a big show whenever I start a new project. I tell people about it and start with special recognition.

- No matter how inconvenient, I will wear my tie clip and write for one-half hour every day for at least two weeks until the new habit against the habit of pro-crastination has been set.

When we conquer the habit of procrastination we become more decisive in solving problems, but we must make sure that we do not just substitute impulsiveness for procrastination. If we remember the rules of preparation in solving problems, we can avoid impulsiveness.

Conquer the Fear of Failure

Why do people delay taking action and hence fail to solve their problems? I think the third reason is fear of failure. Americans are success-oriented people, and we are deathly afraid of what we think are the consequences of failure: rejection, scorn, and being labeled a loser.

Recently in a group therapy class a young lady confessed that she no longer loved her boyfriend. So she went to her boyfriend and told him that she wanted to date other men. He said, "All right, I'll assume that it is over between us." She replied, "No, I want you, but I also want freedom." He answered, "You can't have both." That's how it is with those who want both success and no risk. They want both absolute security and absolute success. You can't have both. Success is predicated upon a certain amount of risk, and you can't have it unless you take that risk.

Dwight D. Eisenhower was commander of the Allied Forces just before the great push into Germany. Every-thing had been considered: the weather; the tides; the posi-tion of the German defense forces; the readiness of troops, ships and supplies. But, in the final analysis, the decision to launch D day was a life and death risk with no certainty of success.

The Allies could have hovered on the English coast, fear-fully awaiting the correct day to launch the invasion. That kind of delay would have been fatal for Western Europe. And it is fatal for those people who allow the fear of failure to run their lives.

One of the most interesting verses in the Bible is found in 2 Timothy 1:7: "God did not give us a spirit of timidity [fearfulness], but a spirit of power, of love and of self-discipline" (NIV). If God did not give us a spirit of fearfulness, where did we get it? Evidently the spirit of fearfulness is foreign to the human body, mind, and spirit because it doesn't come from the Creator. The "spirit of fearfulness" keeps people from making decisions. Here are some ways I use to overcome fear so that I can make a decision.

Consider the fact that a "spirit of fear" is unnatural. Innate fear is one thing. A "spirit of fear" is another. Fear itself comes from God and is used to protect us from harm. Even a baby is born with two innate fears: the fear of falling and the fear of a loud noise. Comedian Steve Allen once joked: "My major fear is that I will make a loud noise while falling."

The "spirit of fear" is a tone of personality that considers the risk more than the benefit. A "spirit of fear" makes decisions based on the fear of consequences rather than possibilities. The person who is guided by a "spirit of fear" is guided by negativism. In the final analysis, a "spirit of fear" turns people into paranoids who are suspicious of everyone and even invent mistrust. So, though fear itself is natural, the "spirit of fear" is unnatural and detrimental. Remember that fact when fear prevents you from making a decision.

The "spirit of fear" can be resisted. True fear is present in every soldier who is confronted with danger, but being guided by the "spirit of fear" turns a soldier into a coward. One soldier said, "Only a fool is not afraid." Bravery means resisting fear and acting brave in spite it. Our war heroes tell us story after story exemplifying the fact that one can be brave when fear descends upon him.

James the apostle said, "Submit yourselves, then, to God. Resist the devil, and he will flee from you" (Jas. 4:7, NIV). And that bit of advice works equally well on fear.

When we resist the "spirit of fear," God gives us special courage as we submit to Him.

Don't let fear take the focus. Fear is a powerful emotion. It will prevent us from taking a risk and making a decision. Fear has a natural purpose: it prevents us from getting hurt and provides us with security. But some people are so afraid of pain that they never can solve the problem of love, and some people are so security conscious that they cling to their home even as a tornado blows it away.

When fear takes the focus, problem-solving stops. As a lad on the edge of that diving board, I was no longer able to solve my problem when I allowed fear to take the focus. On the other hand, when a positive emotion takes the focus, we can forge ahead and take action. First John 4:18 tells us, "Perfect love casts out fear" (NASB). Anyone would be afraid to jump into a raging torrent; but if we see a loved one drowning, fear recedes and love comes to the rescue. If we allow the emotion of love to dictate our decision-making, we will succeed. The positive emotions of faith, hope, and love can take the focus away from fear.

Reach for a Higher Purpose

The last reason I see that keeps people from taking action is lack of a higher purpose. Many times, people do not take action and solve their problems because it doesn't make that much difference to them. Some people are not driven by a magnificent obsession or even by a guiding light. Their lack of being able to see anything higher than themselves prevents them from being motivated to make decisions.

Viktor Frankl was a prisoner in Auschwitz, one of Hitler's concentration camps. He was amazed to see so many people give up their lives without a fight. He discovered that lack of purpose kept many people from fighting for their lives, but those who had a high purpose found a way to live. Viktor Frankl's book, *Man's Search for Meaning*, tells us the story of the development of purpose for life.

We can develop purpose for living, and when we do, decision-making becomes easier. My suggestions for the development of purpose include:

Recognize God's higher power. One-half of the world is guided by the Communistic doctrine that states as a major premise, "There is no God." These people claim to be guided by the greater good of mankind. Even they admit that you must serve someone higher than yourself.

My thought is, why settle for a substitute God? Let God be God. I also believe that our God must represent the highest ideals, the highest integrity, and the highest ethical standards possible. When we pick up the banner of a God who loves us unconditionally and follow the Christlike road, we are on the way toward purposeful living that makes decision-making much easier.

Get your priorities straight. Sometimes people have trouble making decisions because they have not settled on what is right and wrong—they have not arranged a system of priorities. For example, some people in an effort to save their house destroy their home. A home is a relationship between people. A house is merely a place we live. In their eagerness to buy a house, many young couples overextend themselves by working two jobs and seldom see each other. The high rate of divorce can be traced partially to the error of giving up a home for a house. When a couple doesn't take the time to get their priorities straight, they often lose the very thing they are striving for.

Sometimes it is necessary to just sit down and decide what is important. Recently I counseled a man who had been working day and night to provide the fine things of life for his wife and family. His wife served him with divorce papers, claiming he had neglected her and the children. He cried to me, "All I ever wanted was to love my family and be loved. I thought I was doing the right thing." However, he had put his job and making money ahead of relationships. When we get our priorities straight, we develop purpose in life.

Develop your character. A final way to develop purpose in life is to never stop working on developing your character. Character is the strength of purpose to do the right thing. I believe it begins with the firmness of conviction to make little decisions correctly and proceeds until a person is consistent on a high level. We need to spend a lifetime in developing good character; and as we do, we will discover higher and higher purposes for life, and our ability to take action at the proper time will increase.

When Paul the apostle was in Rome awaiting his death, the Bible says he spent his last two years freely speaking about Jesus Christ and the kingdom of God. That was hard work, but Paul never stopped developing his character until he drew his last breath.

One day I walked into an office and saw the desk piled high with mail, papers, and documents. I knew instantly that I was dealing with a person who lacked self-confidence and was having trouble being decisive. This person was in trouble with problem-solving. I knew that I could do something about it because the office and the desk were mine. I was determined to put aside my procrastination. I rolled up my sleeves and decisively handled my mail.

Conclusion

Taking action is dependent upon four factors: choosing to be self-confident, developing the habit of decisiveness by

overcoming the habit of procrastination, developing courage to make a decision by conquering the fear of failure,
and reaching for a higher purpose in life.

One day I walked into an office and saw the desk piled
high with mail, papers, and documents. I knew instantly
that I was dealing with a person who lacked self-confidence
and was having trouble being decisive. This person was in
trouble with problem-solving. I knew that I could do something about it because the office and the desk were mine. I
was determined to put aside my procrastination. I rolled
up my sleeves and decisively handled my mail.

I suggest that we look carefully at how we have organized,
supervised, and deputized our life in terms of decision-making. Is our desk piled high with our procrastinations? If so,
here is my best suggestion to change indecisiveness, disorder, procrastination, and defeat.

Keep a daily planner book and each day choose to be
decisive. Decisiveness is a choice similar to the choices we
make to brush our teeth, comb our hair, and clean our
clothes. We by habit take a shower, shave, and dress. We
by habit can choose to be self-confident, overcome fear, and
develop strong purpose in life.

Remember the bee who was trapped in the house, buzzing against the closed window while striving to get back to
its hive? All it needed to do was back up and fly through
the open door, but it beat itself to death against the windowpane. The decision to back up was probably not within
the bee's system, but praise the Lord it *is* within our system. The human is guided by higher reasoning centers
that can figure things out and make a choice.

We *can* choose. The Creator gave us that ability. What a
wonderful thought. I believe that one of the greatest obstacles to solving problems is indecisiveness. I also believe
that one of the greatest characteristics of a problem-solver
is the ability to take action. The ability to make a decision
is a major hub of problem-solving. We are problem-solvers
to the extent that we are decision-makers.